The
NEW BREED II
by
Gary Chester and Chris Adams

edited by **Rick Mattingly**

Published by
Drummers Intensive Company
P.O. Box 478, 200 Washington Ave., Endicott, NY 13760

Gary Chester
October 27, 1924 - August 17, 1987

To

Gary

This book is dedicated to you, my dear friend. Your Spirit lives on. . .

. . . and The New Breed continues.

Thank you, from all of us.

Acknowledgements

Gary Chester died before the completion of this book. Knowing how much this work meant to him, I graciously accepted the honor and responsibility of seeing it through to the end.

The loving support I received from my family and the entire Gary Chester family helped keep the inspiration alive.

Thank you all:

My Mom and Dad, John and Vicki Adams, whose love and example have taught me the importance of being myself; my brothers, Bill, Tom and John, whose love and support I cherish; Gary's immediate family, especially his wife, Jan, who helped me every step of the way; Gary's daughters, Gayle, Amanda, Jena and Katrina, all so special; his sons, Timmy and Gary Jr. and their families; my aunts, Marie O'Malley and Rosie Calabrese, who are always there for me; my real and dear friends—my drum corps buddies, friends forever; my other very special teacher in life, Norman Grossman, without whose help and guidance I would never have attained the knowledge necessary to write this book; and last, but certainly not least, Gary's extended family—all of his dedicated students, with a gratefully warm thank you to those select few whose support of this project never waned, and whose willingness to continue their work especially helped me in writing this book: David Bell, Robert Bond, Paul Paitchell, Corey Roberts, Mike Ricciardi, and Doreen Holmes; And all the others whose encouragement and support was an extra blessing, thank you: Andy Pastorino, Marc Papazian, Joe Mattis, Adam Hochheiser, Jonathan Lichtig, Kenny Ross, Ed Zacko, Frank Dickerson, Adam Weber, Robert Strobel, Joe Ciano, Mike Marble, Joey Commisso, Jess Wheeler, Alan Johnson, Pete Wilson, Sean Murray, Dave Lazorcik, Mark Frankel, Chris Harfenist, Victor Loyo, John Riley, Ron Tierno, Danny Gottlieb, Clyde Miller, Carol Rupp, the elusive Bobby Kent, and Lee DiClementi.

And my deepest thanks for the loving support and participation of two very special people, Rick Mattingly and Janice Chester.

Thank you all from the bottom of my heart. We've all made this book possible.

Production:
    Chris Adams
    Rick Mattingly

Photography:
    Chris Adams: Cover Photos
    Rick Mattingly: Dedication Photos

Contents

Introduction

The method used in this book will assist you in learning total independence and allow you the freedom to create. As with any form of greatness, patience and perseverance are the keys. You will master anything you set out to master, even the seemingly impossible, with this key formula.

Take your time in learning. Play each part correctly, and make it feel good! It is so important that everything really groove. Use dynamics and sensitivity. Make the melodies sing, and let each drum and cymbal come alive with expression. Sit upright, breathe naturally, relax, and become free of all tension. Your energy will then be good, strong, and ready to flow. Pay attention to yourself and to the sounds you are creating. Focus. Become aware of each part you are playing. Sing each part. Hear each part separately, then all together as one.

Stay with each exercise until it is mastered—until it is played accurately and with a great feel. Completely satisfy yourself before moving on to something new. It's not important how fast you get through this book, but how thoroughly these developed skills become a part of you. Rome wasn't built in a day, nor will this concept become automatic in a week or a month. But eventually the skills learned from this method will become a standard part of your everyday musical vocabulary. This will allow you the freedom to create anything that you hear or feel.

It's hard work, probably the most difficult independence exercises ever written for drummers. And because of this, it's challenging, stimulating, and rewarding.

Welcome to the advanced studies of *The New Breed*.

from Gary. . .

"There are no limits to learning. If you are good, you strive to be better. If you are better, you strive to be fantastic. If you are fantastic, you want greatness. And so on. It all depends on how hungry you are and to what limits you will go.

Everyone has ambition, but what are you putting into the instrument that you expect greatness to come out of? Everyone hopes to become good, but is that good enough?

*This brings us to the fact that a musician needs internal motivation to want to achieve satisfaction and have a feeling of accomplishment and pride. Remember, you are calling the shots. Once you lose your motivation, or let someone or something distract you away from it, you're in trouble. You're doing this for yourself and to yourself. You're practicing to please someone else in a performance situation, but before all this you must satisfy **yourself**.*

Which brings us to your confidence. You must know that you are capable of handling any situation necessary..."

This is where Gary has left us—to begin. Everything necessary to help you develop the skills, the confidence, and the motivation needed to satisfy you is in this book. It's all up to you.

Where We Begin

Trust: as defined in the Funk & Wagnalls Standard Desk Dictionary, 1. A confident reliance on the integrity, honesty, or justice of another; faith.... 4. to allow to do something without fear of consequences.

Self trust is where we begin. It's that inner sense of trusting oneself that starts the ball rolling. Without self trust, there would be no self confidence, and without that confidence, one might never step out to move towards one's goals. Without that forward motion, one could never strive to reach his or her potential.

So trust is where it all begins, but what exactly does that mean, and how do we learn to trust ourselves? Well, first we must learn to *pay attention*. We all have needs, wants, desires, and instincts. By allowing ourselves to hear and feel those things inside us, by paying close attention, we begin to know ourselves. And that knowledge contains everything we need to know, including a strong sense of right and wrong. In knowing this, we can each begin to journey towards what is right for us. With this knowledge comes a sense of *trust* in pursuing that which is right.

Gary used to say that this method is not for everyone; neither is drumming or a career in music, for that matter. But if your instincts have led you here, then it's up to you to follow the road ahead and stay on course.

After awareness and self trust come patience and perseverance—valuable keys necessary to reach one's goals. But what are your goals? Each of us has our own goals that are as individual as each person. Your goal could be as specific as a definite career achievement, or just a desire to improve yourself each day. Defining your goals, both short- and long-term, will help you set your course.

Patience is so necessary. As individuals, we work and grow quite differently, each of our lives being entirely unique. You can't set your pace according to someone else's. You can't judge yourself or your abilities by comparing yourself to someone else. You must work with what you have, and with that understanding and acceptance comes patience. Whether you work a little bit everyday or a lot, or work in spurts and then rest (accomplishing milestones and then taking time to digest it, so to speak), it's crucial for you to learn, know, and understand *your own pace* and patiently allow it.

To persevere means to continue, to persist, to strive—even in spite of difficulties. Life is amazing and full of surprises. Even with patience and understanding, nature dictates change—from blue skies to hurricanes—yet we continue. Perseverance is an important and necessary ingredient. Without it we stop: stop learning, stop growing. We all have potential, but to reach that potential we must keep learning and keep growing our entire lives.

So learn to **listen**—first to what's inside. In learning to listen to ourselves, we can then understand how to listen to others.
Learn to **trust**—first yourself. In learning self trust we learn how to trust others.
Learn **patience.** Learn to walk in step with *yourself,* and to allow nature to guide you. Walk with the wind, not against it. In learning patience with ourselves, we learn to have patience with others.
Learn to **persevere**—to continue, to strive. In learning how to persevere, we learn how to help others do the same.
And learn to **love.** Love yourself, your path, your life. It's all a part of you. In learning to love ourselves, we allow ourselves to love and appreciate the beauty in others, and allow ourselves to be loved and appreciated by others.

In starting from within ourselves, we gain a very deep understanding of self, of life, and of others. The most beautiful music is created with a blend of all of this. It's something too precious to miss.

This book was written with love, trust, patience, and perseverance, as was Gary's creation of this method. We offer it in the sincere hope that it may continue to open doors for those who wish to go beyond the norm, and to reach the hidden potentials that are inside, just waiting to be tapped.

IMPORTANT MESSAGE...

This Is A Very Advanced Book

Not everyone will be able to jump right in at this level. If, after attempting the first few Bonuses with their recommended Melodies, you find that this book begins at a level of difficulty beyond your present abilities, begin with Gary's first book, *The New Breed*, published by Modern Drummer. Master all of the Systems in that book with all of the Melodies. You'll then be ready to begin this sequel. Or, use this book as a supplement to the first one.

There is no set time period in which you should go through either book. Take your time, but work hard. Tape yourself regularly. Notice and enjoy your progress. There will be certain Systems or Bonuses that will almost seem impossible at first. You'll feel stuck, frustrated, and maybe even angry or helpless for a while, but *be patient.* You'll need to take it one step at a time—maybe one beat at a time, then one bar, then one line, and so on. *We've all been there!* It's those who slowly persevere who rise to great heights.

It's up to you to develop the skills necessary to create the music of the future.

Follow All Instructions

Gary developed this unique method for the advancement of a truly New Breed of drummers. Although the Systems and Bonuses are quite complex, the method itself is direct, practical, and endlessly interchangeable.

It is essential that you understand how to use the book if you are to benefit from it fully. *Pay close attention to all instructions* and do everything as instructed, including singing, until you have mastered it. If there are any instructions that you don't fully understand, take the time to reread them and follow them step by step.

You'll find a Glossary at the end of the book that defines some of the frequently used terms.

Practice all exercises in this book with a metronome. Always begin slowly, around quarter-note = 60, and once you have mastered an exercise at a slow tempo, try various tempos.

Drum Setup

Feeling centered behind your drumset is important. However, it is not totally necessary that you have two X-hats or two floor toms to begin practicing this method. It is desirable, but if you don't have X-hats, position ride cymbals on your right and left sides and play the X-hat parts on these cymbals. You should muffle the cymbals for more defintion while practicing.

On the bonuses that require the use of a left-side floor tom, you can substitute any extra mounted tom.

If you have any comments about this book, or would like information about studying Gary's method with Chris Adams through cassette corespondence, write to: Chris Adams, Drummers Intensive, P.O. Box 478, 200 Washington Ave., Endicott NY 13760.

BONUSES, MELODIES, AND PATTERNS

Bonuses

Important: Read everything thoroughly and follow all instructions

This is a sequel to Gary Chester's first book and contains some of his most difficult exercises, which he called Bonuses. There are over 50 of them in this book, and they all vary, so in addition to the general instructions given here you must look carefully at each Bonus for more specific information.

To the left of each Bonus are abbreviations that indicate which instrument to play on (SN, BD, HH, etc.), which hand or foot to use (RH, LF, etc.), and which part to play (Melody, Pattern, etc.). Study these carefully, as this is the key information for each Bonus.

The Bonuses are subdivided into groups using such titles as Sock Talks, Broken, Wac-a-Chuck, Cross, etc. Each group of Bonuses lists a suggested Melody to work with when practicing that particular group. It is recommended that you begin with the suggested Melody and its Warm-ups, as certain Melodies work better with certain Bonuses.

Work on only one Bonus and its suggested melody at a time.

Work at your drumkit with a metronome or drum machine click pulse. It is recommended that you do this *without* the use of headphones so that you can hear everything you are playing as well as the click. Try using the metronome or drum machine amplified through speakers.

Once you have mastered a Bonus with the suggested melody, you can then try playing that Bonus with *any* of the other Melodies, including the Bonus Melodies, for extra practice. Another approach would be to first master all of the Bonuses with their suggested Melodies, and then begin again using Melodies of your choice.

This concept also applies to the Patterns used with each Bonus. After mastering all of the Bonuses with the Patterns given, begin again using different patterns. Pick patterns from the listing at the end of this section or make up your own.

This should give you an idea of how interchangeable Gary's method is, and what a wonderful life-long challenge it can present.

General instructions for all of the Bonuses follow, but be sure to also observe any additional instructions given with each Bonus or group of Bonuses.

The following abbreviations are used in this book:

HH	Hi-hat		RH	Right hand
XH	X-hat (auxiliary closed hi-hat)		LH	Left hand
Bell	Bell of cymbal		RF	Right foot
Ride	Ride cymbal		LF	Left Foot
BD	Bass drum			
SN	Snare drum			
FT	Floor tom			
Toms	High to low toms			
Rim	Cross-stick on snare			

Examples:

XH	RH	Rests of Pat.	(Play Rests of Pattern with Right Hand on X-Hat)
Toms	LH	Melody	(Play Melody with Left Hand on any Toms around kit.)
Bell	RH	Upbeats	(Play Upbeats with Right Hand on Bell of Cymbal.)
SN	RH	Pattern	(Play Pattern with Right Hand on Snare Drum)

BOUNS INSTRUCTIONS

Shown below is a Bonus as it appears in Section 1.

1. XH	RH	RESTS of PAT.
SN	LH	PATTERN
BD	RF	**MELODY**
HH	LF	UPBEATS

Following are the steps involved in mastering the Bonus.

STEP 1

Begin with Bonus #1.
Study all information given in Bonus and Key.
Set click to quarter note = 60.

STEP 2

Play all Patterns, including Upbeats and Rests of Patterns where indicated. Notice where you will eventually play the Melody, but DO NOT PLAY MELODY YET.
Play this over and over, accurately and relaxed. Lock into Time.

STEP 3

As you play these parts, SING the Quarter Notes (click). This means to sing rhythmically ALOUD. DO NOT COUNT NUMBERS. Find a sound that feels comfortable to you and sing that. You can mimic the sound of the click, or as you get into singing other parts, imitate the sound of the instrument each part is being played on.

Example: Singing the Quarter Notes (click).

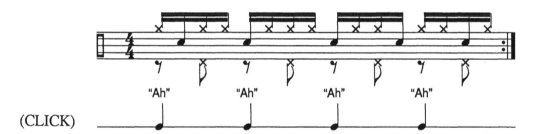

(CLICK)

Next, SING EACH PATTERN or part that you are playing. Make a firm imprint in your mind of the part that you're singing. Be sure that your playing and singing are exactly together. Take your time here. Play the Bonus repeatedly, singing each part over and over, as many times as it takes for you to become completely familiar with that part.

Example: Singing Snare Pattern   Singing Upbeats

STEP 4

When you have memorized these parts, TURN TO THE MELODY WARM-UPS for the suggested Melody given for that Bonus. (You'll find the Melody number to turn to in the upper left corner of the page each Bonus is on. You'll find the cooresponding Melody Warm-ups on the page before the Melody.)

While playing the Bonus you have just memorized, ADD THE MELODY WARM-UPS, one by one. Refer to Bonus Key for specifics as to where to play the Melody. (In the above Example, you would play Melody with Right Foot on Bass Drum.)

Repeat each Warm-Up many times before moving on to the next. Once you have mastered the Warm-Ups, you are ready to TURN TO THE MELODY. Again, while playing the memorized Bonus, PLAY THE ENTIRE TWO-PAGE MELODY from beginning to end.

Below is an example of playing all the parts together.

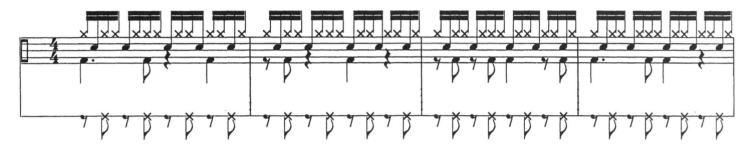

The independence required here can be extremely difficult; however, if you work slowly, using patience and perseverance, you'll get it! Work at your own pace, bar by bar, stopping and starting as needed, until finally you can play the entire Melody, while playing all of the other parts, without stopping.

STEP 5

Once you've acquired this independence, REPEAT MANY TIMES! Each time you play the Bonus with the entire Melody, SING a different part that you are playing, as well as singing the quarter notes. This will now include singing the Melody.

Example:

First	SING	QUARTER NOTES (CLICK)
Next	SING	UPBEATS
Next	SING	PATTERN (sing each pattern if there are more than one)
Next	SING	MELODY
Next	SING	RESTS (sing Rests of Pattern or Melody if any are being played)

Focus on the part that you are singing. HEAR IT. PLAY IT. SING IT. SEE IT in alignment with all the other parts that you are playing.

IMPORTANT: Don't stop at just getting the independence. Although this alone is quite an accomplishment, good is not good enough! You must be able to play each Bonus with the entire Melody accurately and with a great feel, as if to make your instrument dance—with proper execution, yet relaxed and flowing.

This will require playing each Bonus with the Melody many, many times. Each time singing a different part and making it groove just a little more. Only then will you be able to learn, retain and use a brilliantly new musical vocabulary.

As your skills improve, try various tempos. Some drummers will question, or want to ignore, the Bonuses that lead with the left hand. This is a dangerous temptation. Just do them! The balance and independence skills this will lead to are second to none.

12

Broken

♩ = 60

melody 1

MEMORIZE PATTERNS
TURN TO WARM-UPS/MELODY
PLAY PATTERNS WITH MELODY

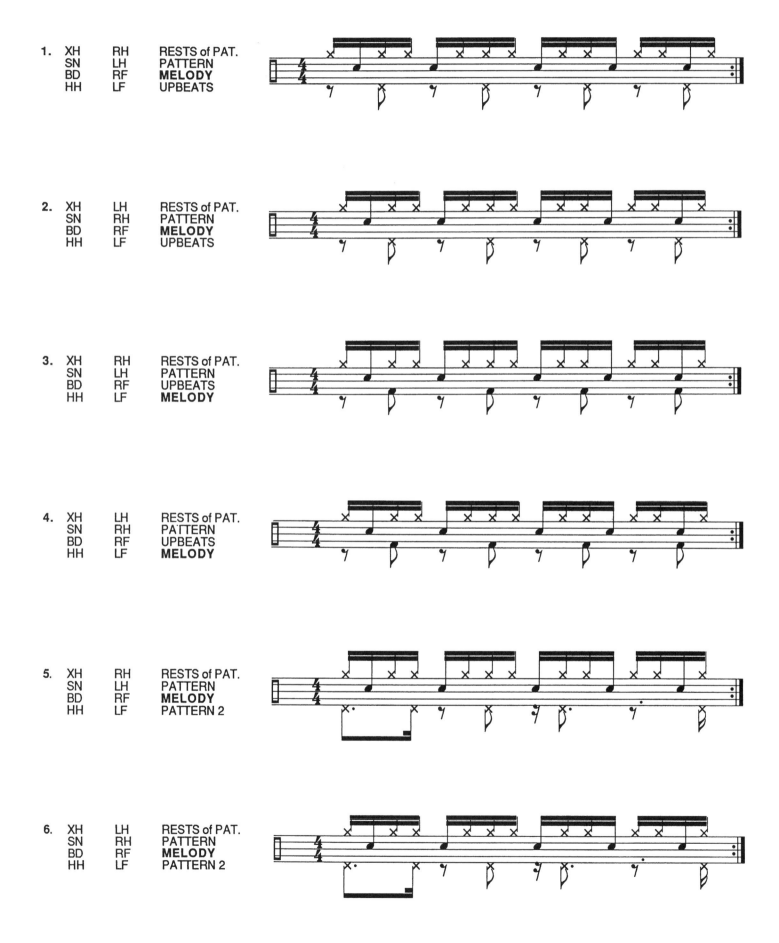

1. XH RH RESTS of PAT.
    SN LH PATTERN
    BD RF **MELODY**
    HH LF UPBEATS

2. XH LH RESTS of PAT.
    SN RH PATTERN
    BD RF **MELODY**
    HH LF UPBEATS

3. XH RH RESTS of PAT.
    SN LH PATTERN
    BD RF UPBEATS
    HH LF **MELODY**

4. XH LH RESTS of PAT.
    SN RH PATTERN
    BD RF UPBEATS
    HH LF **MELODY**

5. XH RH RESTS of PAT.
    SN LH PATTERN
    BD RF **MELODY**
    HH LF PATTERN 2

6. XH LH RESTS of PAT.
    SN RH PATTERN
    BD RF **MELODY**
    HH LF PATTERN 2

Cross
♩ = 60
melody 2

ALTERNATE STICKING
(RH on R. XH, LH on L. XH)
MEMORIZE PATTERNS
TURN TO WARM-UPS/MELODY
PLAY PATTERNS WITH MELODY

7. XH'S   R&LH   RESTS of PAT.
   SN   R&LH   PATTERN
   BD   RF   **MELODY**
   HH   LF   UPBEATS

8. XH'S   L&RH   RESTS of PAT.
   SN   L&RH   PATTERN
   BD   RF   **MELODY**
   HH   LF   UPBEATS

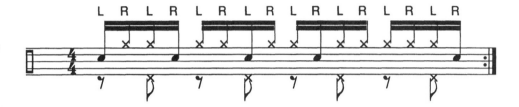

9. XH'S   R&LH   **RESTS of MEL.**
   SN   R&LH   **MELODY**
   BD   RF   PATTERN
   HH   LF   UPBEATS

10. XH'S   L&RH   **RESTS of MEL.**
   SN   L&RH   **MELODY**
   BD   RF   PATTERN
   HH   LF   UPBEATS

11. XH'S   R&LH   RESTS of PAT.
   TOMS R&LH   PATTERN
   BD   RF   **MELODY**
   HH   LF   UPBEATS

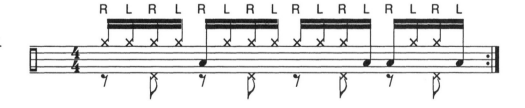

12. XH'S   L&RH   RESTS of PAT.
   TOMS L&RH   PATTERN
   BD   RF   **MELODY**
   HH   LF   UPBEATS

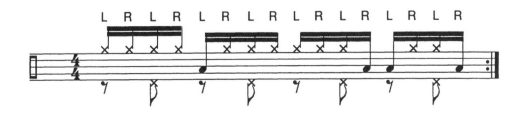

14

Wac-A-Chuck

♩ = 60
melody 3

MEMORIZE PATTERNS
TURN TO WARM-UPS/MELODY
PLAY PATTERNS WITH MELODY

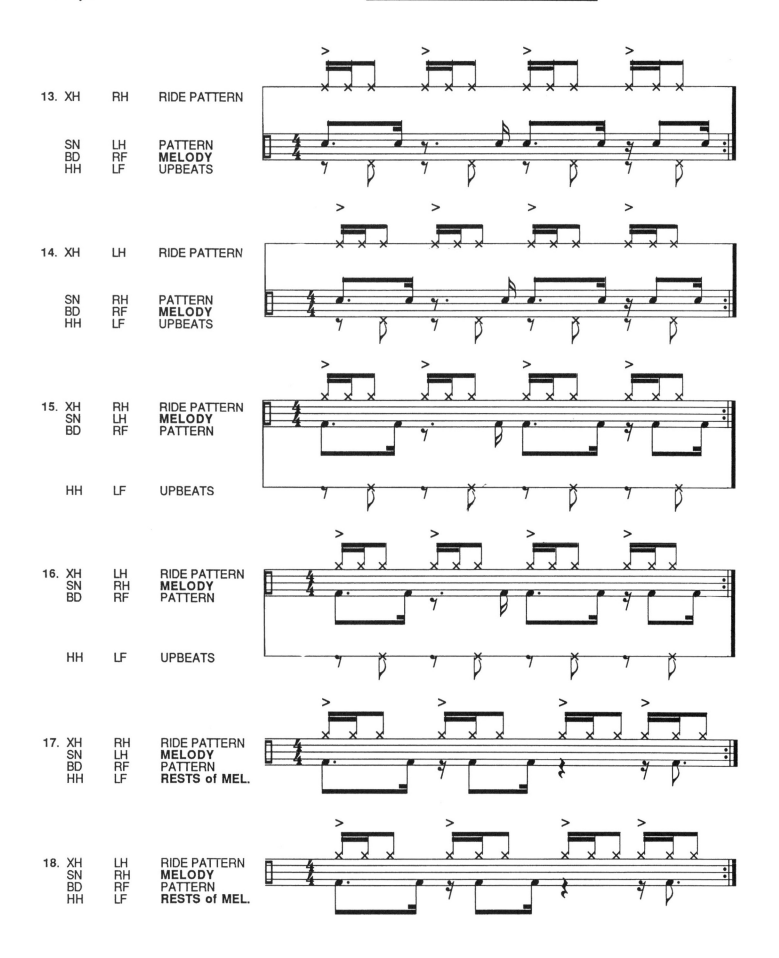

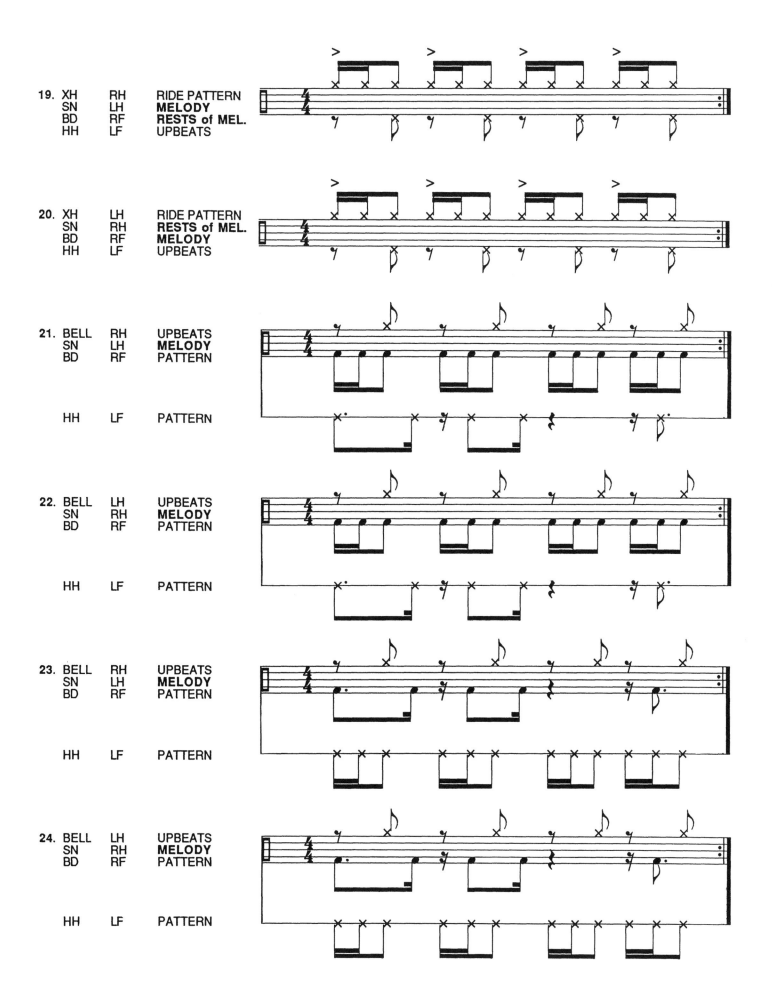

16

Reverse Wac-A-Chuck

♩ = 60
melody 2

MEMORIZE PATTERNS
TURN TO WARM-UPS/MELODY
PLAY PATTERNS WITH MELODY

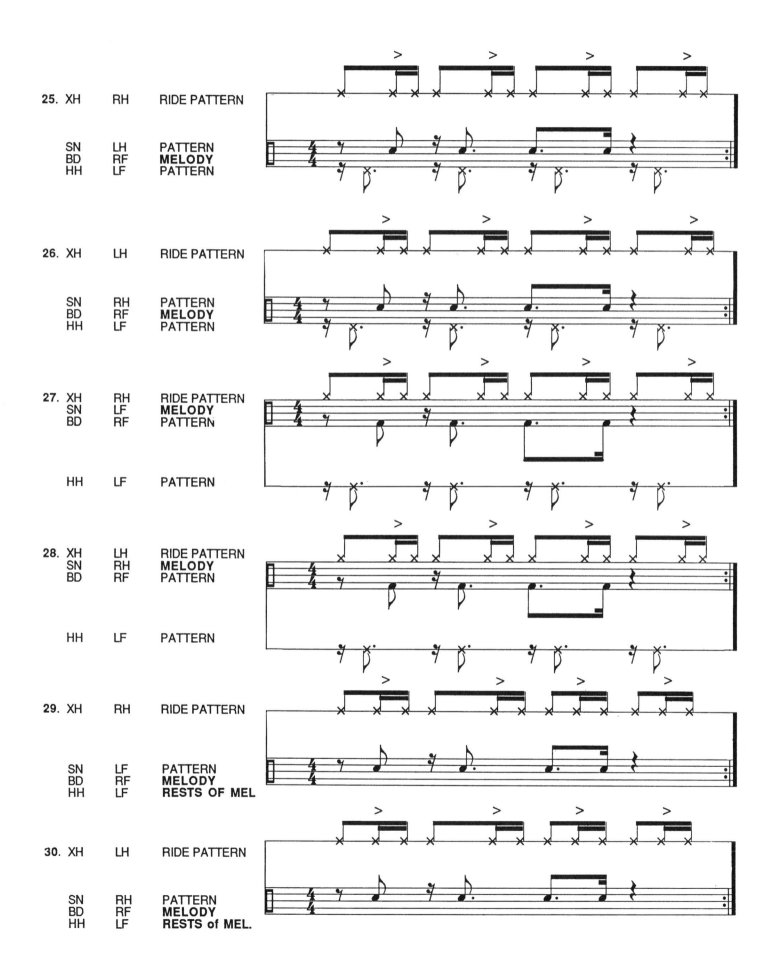

Sock Talks

♩ = 60
melody 3

MEMORIZE PATTERNS
TURN TO WARM-UPS/MELODY
PLAY PATTERNS WITH MELODY

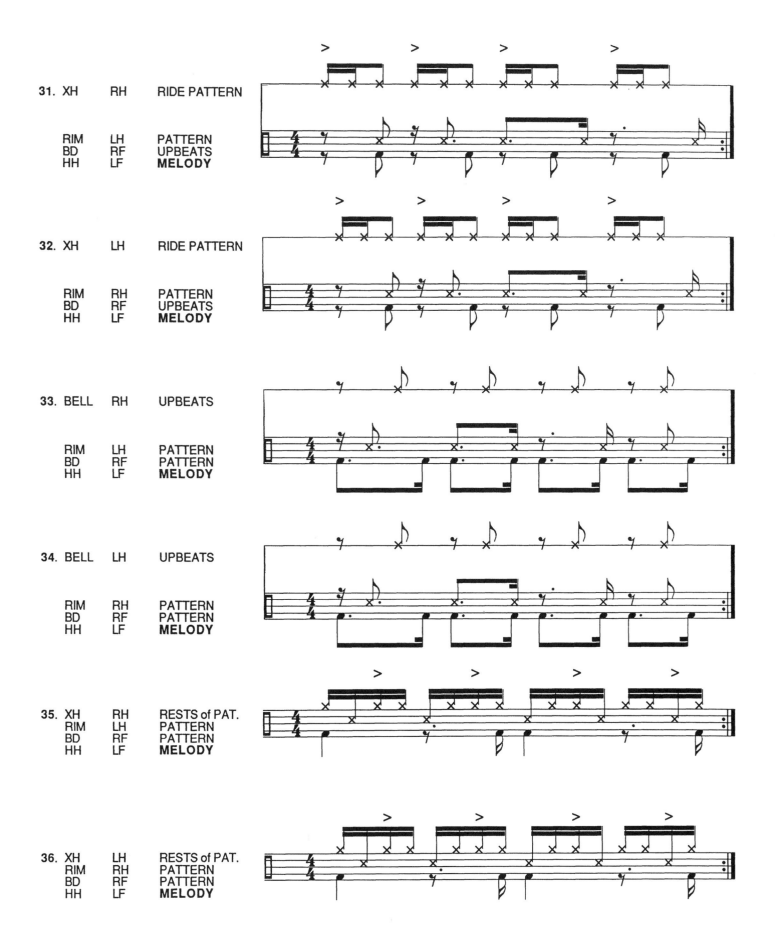

31.	XH	RH	RIDE PATTERN
	RIM	LH	PATTERN
	BD	RF	UPBEATS
	HH	LF	**MELODY**

32.	XH	LH	RIDE PATTERN
	RIM	RH	PATTERN
	BD	RF	UPBEATS
	HH	LF	**MELODY**

33.	BELL	RH	UPBEATS
	RIM	LH	PATTERN
	BD	RF	PATTERN
	HH	LF	**MELODY**

34.	BELL	LH	UPBEATS
	RIM	RH	PATTERN
	BD	RF	PATTERN
	HH	LF	**MELODY**

35.	XH	RH	RESTS of PAT.
	RIM	LH	PATTERN
	BD	RF	PATTERN
	HH	LF	**MELODY**

36.	XH	LH	RESTS of PAT.
	RIM	RH	PATTERN
	BD	RF	PATTERN
	HH	LF	**MELODY**

Playing the Rests

♩ = 60
melody 4

MEMORIZE PATTERNS
TURN TO WARM-UPS/MELODY
PLAY PATTERNS WITH MELODY

37. XH   RH   **RESTS of MEL.**
    SN   LH   **MELODY**
    BD   RF   PATTERN
    HH   LF   UPBEATS

38. XH   LH   **RESTS of MEL.**
    SN   RH   **MELODY**
    BD   RF   PATTERN
    HH   LF   UPBEATS

39. BELL RH   UPBEATS
    SN   LH   **MELODY**
    BD   RF   PATTERN
    HH   LF   **RESTS of MEL.**

40. BELL LH   UPBEATS
    SN   RH   **MELODY**
    BD   RF   PATTERN
    HH   LF   **RESTS of MEL.**

41. BELL RH   UPBEATS
    SN   LH   PATTERN
    BD   RF   **MELODY**
    HH   LF   **RESTS of MEL.**

42. BELL LH   UPBEATS
    SN   RH   PATTERN
    BD   RF   **RESTS of MEL.**
    HH   LF   **MELODY**

Double Broken

♩ = 60
melody 5

MEMORIZE PATTERNS
TURN TO WARM-UPS/MELODY
PLAY PATTERNS WITH MELODY

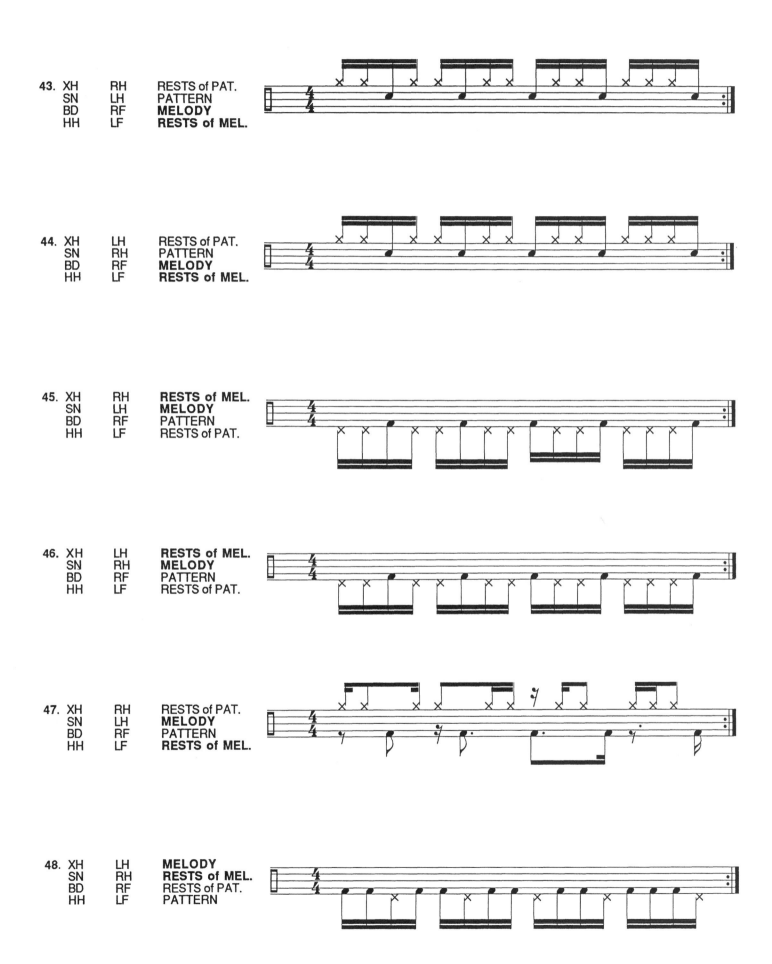

43. XH RH RESTS of PAT.
    SN LH PATTERN
    BD RF **MELODY**
    HH LF **RESTS of MEL.**

44. XH LH RESTS of PAT.
    SN RH PATTERN
    BD RF **MELODY**
    HH LF **RESTS of MEL.**

45. XH RH **RESTS of MEL.**
    SN LH **MELODY**
    BD RF PATTERN
    HH LF RESTS of PAT.

46. XH LH **RESTS of MEL.**
    SN RH **MELODY**
    BD RF PATTERN
    HH LF RESTS of PAT.

47. XH RH RESTS of PAT.
    SN LH **MELODY**
    BD RF PATTERN
    HH LF **RESTS of MEL.**

48. XH LH **MELODY**
    SN RH **RESTS of MEL.**
    BD RF RESTS of PAT.
    HH LF PATTERN

Disco

♩ = 60
bonus melody 1

THINK MELODIC/TOMS
MEMORIZE PATTERNS
TURN TO WARM-UPS/MELODY
PLAY PATTERNS WITH MELODY

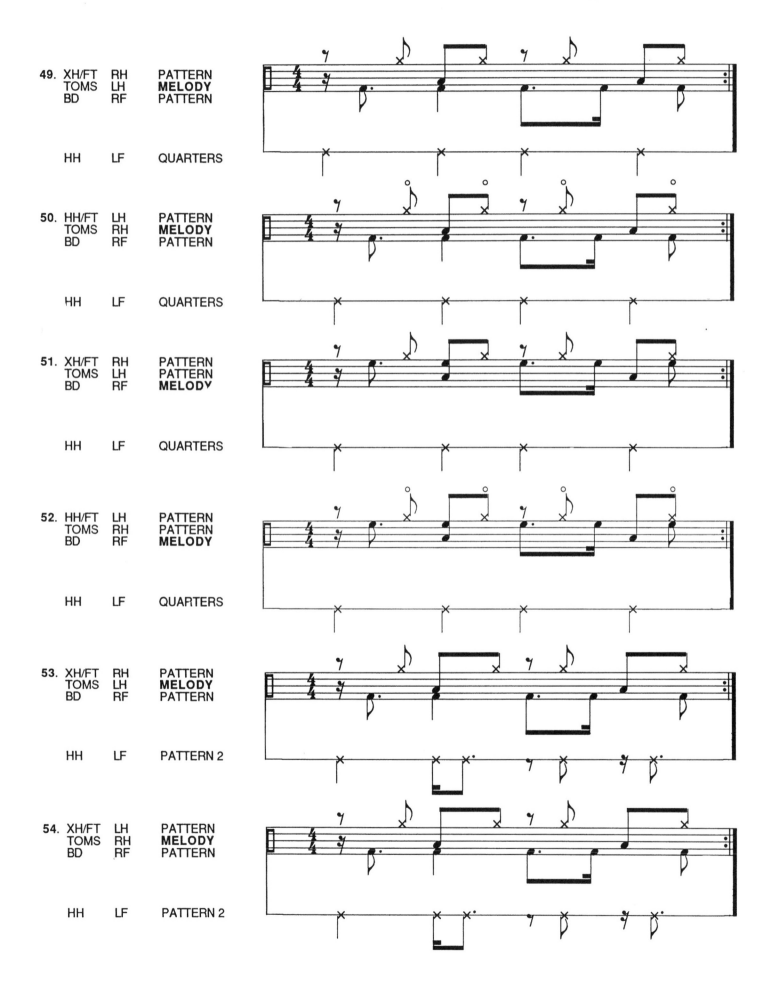

Funk Swing

♩ = 60
bonus melody 2

PLAY WITH SWING FEEL
MEMORIZE PATTERN
TURN TO WARM-UPS/MELODY
PLAY PATTERNS WITH MELODY

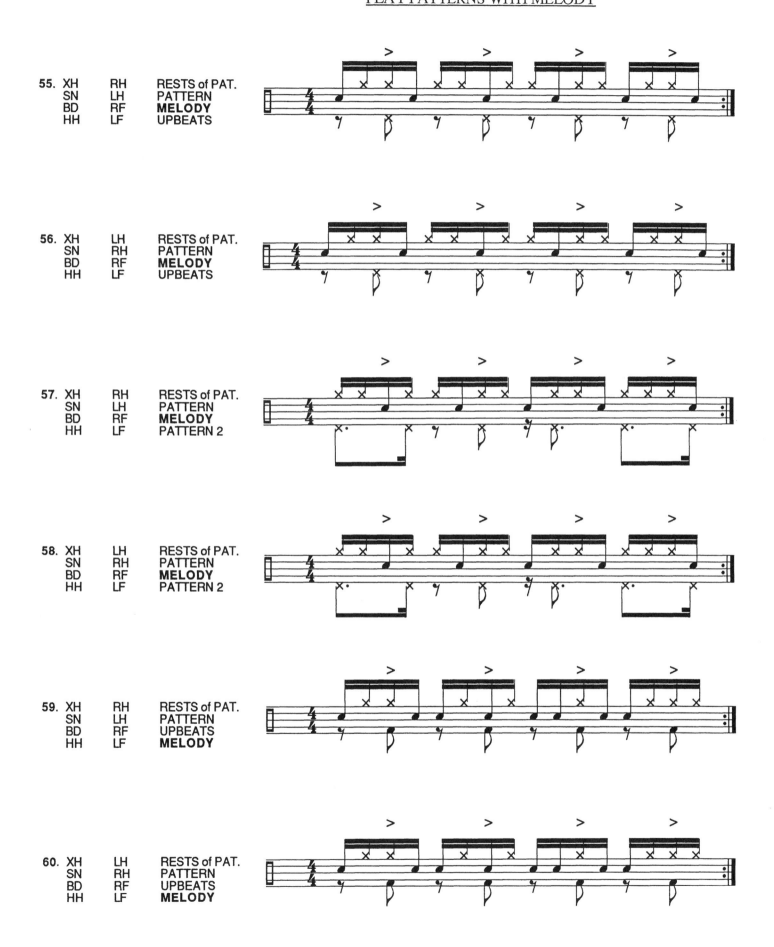

55.	XH	RH	RESTS of PAT.
	SN	LH	PATTERN
	BD	RF	**MELODY**
	HH	LF	UPBEATS

56.	XH	LH	RESTS of PAT.
	SN	RH	PATTERN
	BD	RF	**MELODY**
	HH	LF	UPBEATS

57.	XH	RH	RESTS of PAT.
	SN	LH	PATTERN
	BD	RF	**MELODY**
	HH	LF	PATTERN 2

58.	XH	LH	RESTS of PAT.
	SN	RH	PATTERN
	BD	RF	**MELODY**
	HH	LF	PATTERN 2

59.	XH	RH	RESTS of PAT.
	SN	LH	PATTERN
	BD	RF	UPBEATS
	HH	LF	**MELODY**

60.	XH	LH	RESTS of PAT.
	SN	RH	PATTERN
	BD	RF	UPBEATS
	HH	LF	**MELODY**

22

Funk Swing (Two Bar Patterns)

♩ = 60
bonus melody 3

PLAY WITH SWING FEEL
MEMORIZE PATTERNS
TURN TO WARM-UPS/MELODY
PLAY PATTERNS WITH MELODY

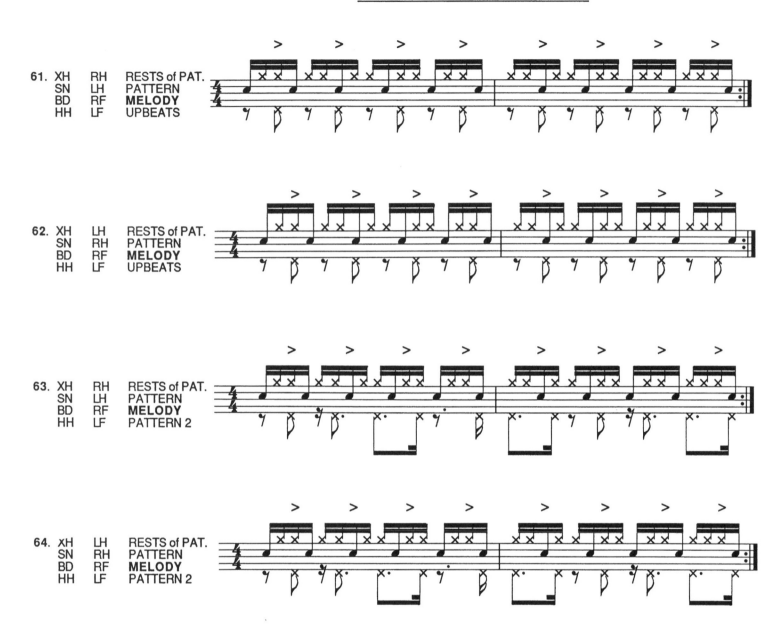

61.	XH	RH	RESTS of PAT.
	SN	LH	PATTERN
	BD	RF	**MELODY**
	HH	LF	UPBEATS

62.	XH	LH	RESTS of PAT.
	SN	RH	PATTERN
	BD	RF	**MELODY**
	HH	LF	UPBEATS

63.	XH	RH	RESTS of PAT.
	SN	LH	PATTERN
	BD	RF	**MELODY**
	HH	LF	PATTERN 2

64.	XH	LH	RESTS of PAT.
	SN	RH	PATTERN
	BD	RF	**MELODY**
	HH	LF	PATTERN 2

The Internal Quarter Note

Gary's Method trains us to use more of our minds than we normally do in most areas of life. It teaches us to develop skills so finely and imprint them so thoroughly in our minds that we can use more of our conscious energy elsewhere and know that the unconscious mind is trained and can be trusted. So we can be assured of skillful execution and learn to really relax, leaving the conscious mind open and free to explore—the groundwork for true creativity.

Gary understood this, which motivated him to stress the importance of studying his Method to serious students. He was excited by the level of excellence it created, and that excitement is something he left us.

Gary's Method is the most challenging and rewarding study of drumming I have ever undertaken.

"It's taking the mechanical step and going beyond."

Listed before each melody are some common melody figures that make excellent warm-ups. Begin slowly and master these bars with each bonus. Repeat each one many times, then proceed to the appropriate melody.

warm-ups for melodies 1 & 2

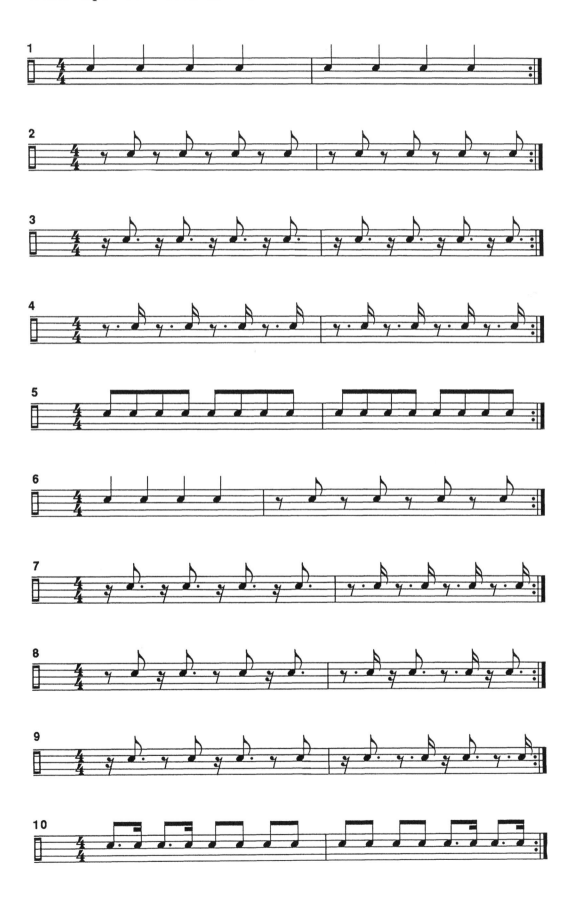

Melody 1

Melody 2

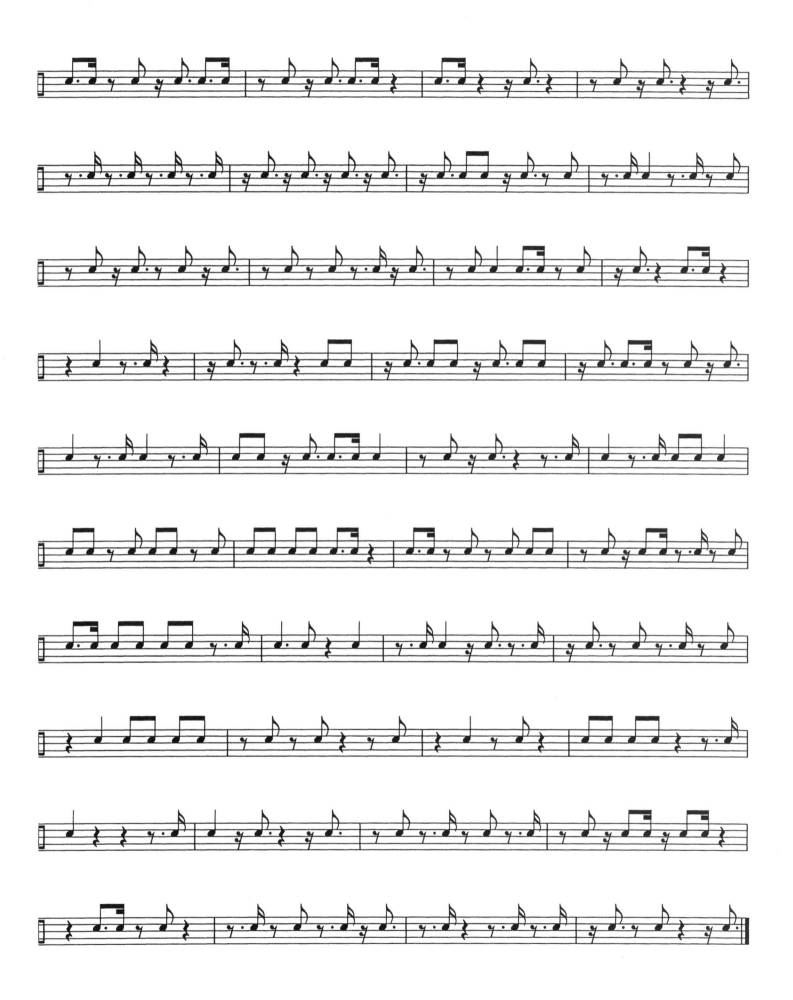

"This book is designed to make you more aware of what you are hearing and playing. Singing each part that each of your limbs play will train your ears to accept and understand what you're doing. When you have mastered this, then and only then can you hear what you are saying on your instrument."

"A lot of things happen to musicians to mold their personalities. Disappointments are a must, so that you can learn to turn a disadvantage into an advantage."

"Meeting all sorts of people goes hand in hand with this business. You live on promises until you are forced to take a stand."

"There are so many facets of this art/business. You don't have to be famous to have gone through all of them, but you must go through all types of musical experiences."

"The emotional abuse a musician takes just to prove himself to himself, this is what makes a musician. He takes pride in his instrument; he takes pride in his self discipline."

"In the studio, you have to marry the bass player. The bass drum must do one of three things:
1. play exactly what the bass plays
2. stay out of his way
3. complement him."

"...and Time—time is the master of things! It's the most important thing. Beyond that is Attitude—attitude is the next most important thing."

warm-ups for melody 3

Melody 3

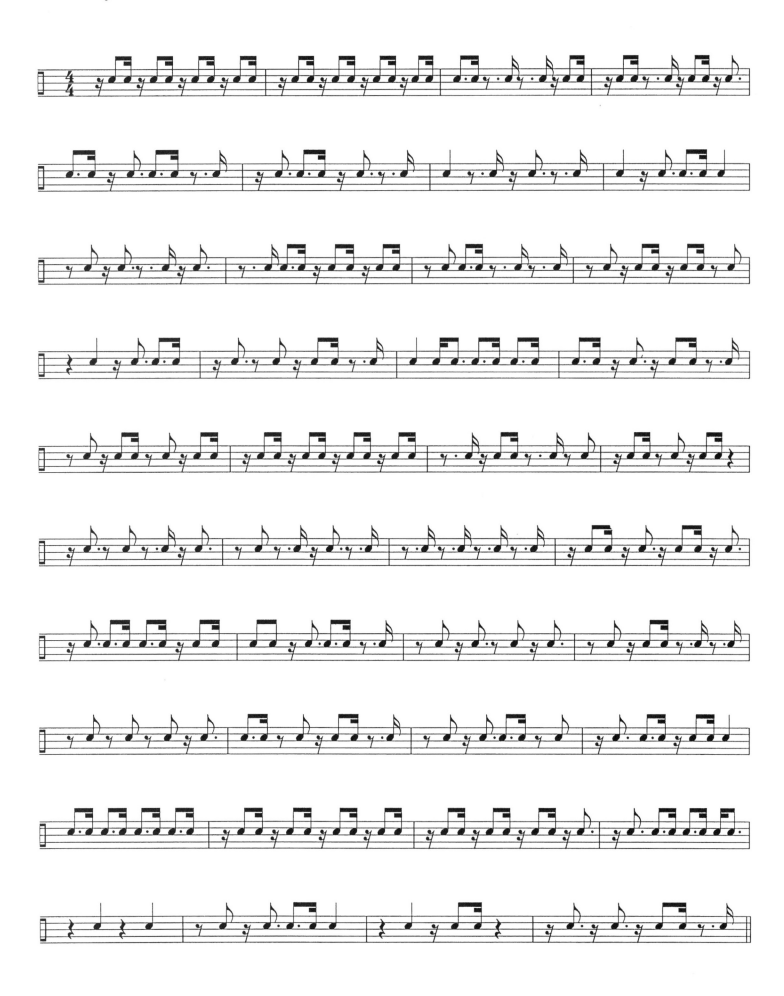

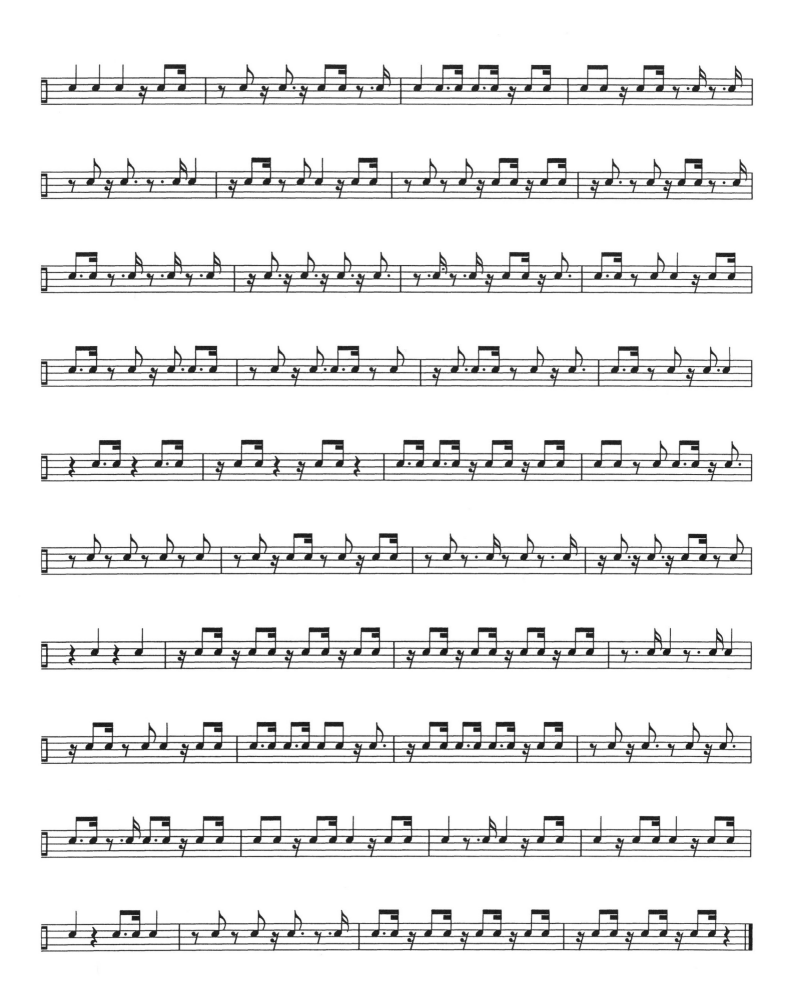

"Did you ever notice how many musicians sound alike? It's like top-40 lounge bands, who all copy the same records. These days, when you audition for a band, they send you a tape so that you can mimic their previous drummer. If you don't play the same fills, you're out, and the guy who can, gets the job (if there is one).

"A long time ago, auditions were a lot different. You went in and played with enthusiasm—you played your best. They paid attention to your reading skills, your time, and your concept of the things you were reading. Even if you didn't read so well, but could carry the band, they were content. It left a lot of room to create. But today, there's no room to create, only to copy. That only does one thing for a drummer—it causes frustration.

"Five out of ten drummers who 'made it' aren't good musicians; they just got a break. That's sad. But they'll never advance, because in this business, when you stop learning, you're old hat. Remember, it's hard to get there, but it's twice as hard to stay there."

"There are different kinds of musicians. There are some who have to be 'stars.' They're usually the speed freaks who don't read, play fast, and make a big impression. But the guy who will make the money is the guy who is willing to take a back seat and make another artist sound good, in the studio, or in fact in every part of life."

"In 1940, we played ding ding-a-ding with one bass line, and we thought we were great! But today, you have to be able to read four lines at once, and that's very important. See, some people don't grow. They do the same thing that this guy did or that guy did, and they die."

warm-ups for melody 4

Melody 4

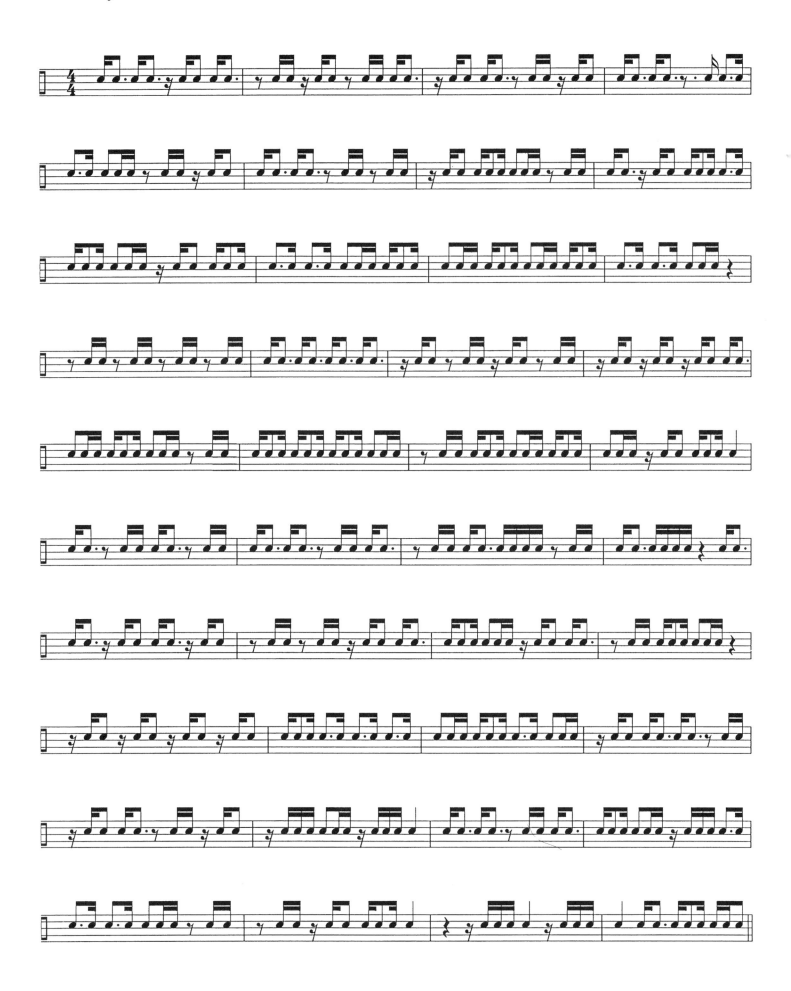

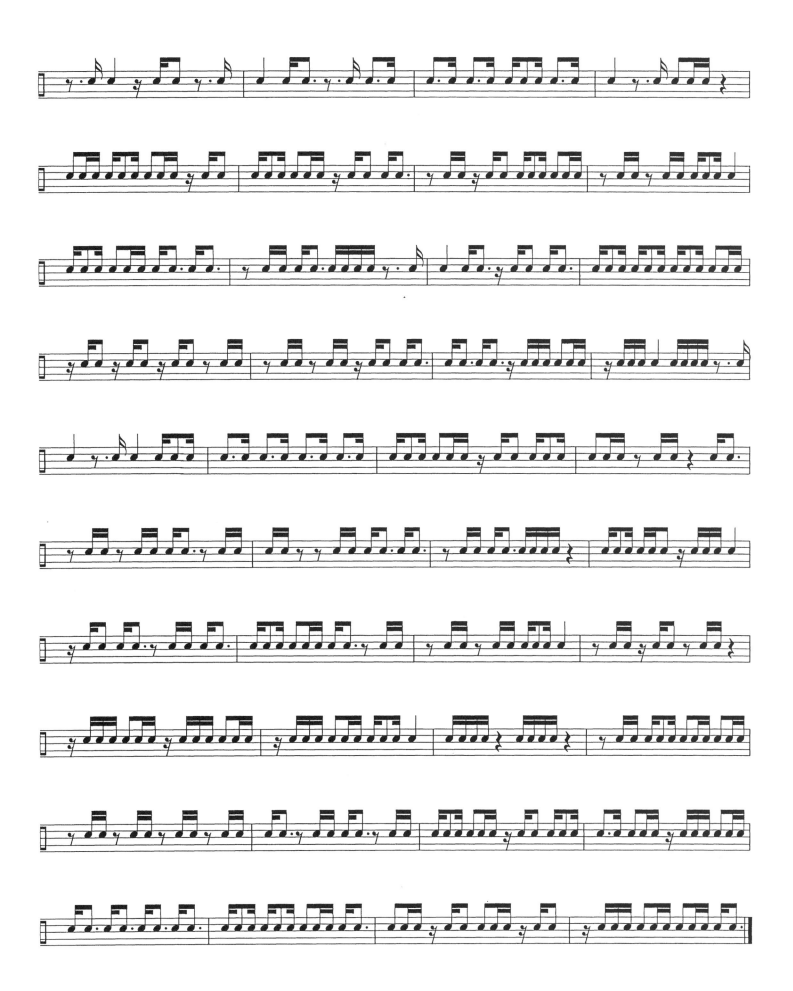

"I want you to realize how difficult it is—how much we have to learn. And that's what this method does for you: it makes you aware of what you can't do, so that you can better yourself."

"You can go out and play a gig, and everyone can say, 'Wow, what a great drummer,' but that really doesn't count. What really counts is that you play good and you know you play good. And you know what went on in the band—when someone was dragging, when someone was out of tune. Your ears are alert. You hear what your left foot is doing, what your right foot is doing, your eyes are relating to the music, and you're doing everything the way that you want to do it."

"There are three things you must have to become successful:
*First is the **desire** for success.*
*Second is the **motivation** to do what you're told to do.*
*Third is the **goal** to be able to accomplish all of this."*

"This is what Zen Buddhism is about as far as drumming is concerned. It's not the drumset, it's not the sticks, it's all you. So as soon as you see something, it comes right out through your body."

"You probably wonder, 'Why do I have to sing?' Well, that's the only way you are going to relate to your playing. When you're singing the bass drum part, you're imitating the sound, and you're hearing the bass drum. It's imbedded in your head and you know exactly what you're playing. It's the same thing when you sing the melody, or the quarter-note pulse."

"There are three kinds of time:
1. on time
2. behind time
3. on top (ahead) of time.
The three of them have to be mastered—by you."

"Guys think they have good right hands, but what they really have is a good left side feeding the right."

"When muscles are out of balance, it's natural for them to freeze up and affect the flow of time execution. Nervousness will often cause this hesitation in playing. Being balanced on your drumset and breathing correctly can help you avoid the tension.

"If you think of practicing as developing the muscles, you will eliminate the nervousness and hesitation in your playing. Think of the Systems as muscle builders. Remember, before anything can groove, it must feel good body-wise. The muscles have to be trained and stretched slowly in order for you to make them do what you want them to do."

"I'm trying to take away the mediocrity of today's drummers and bring them up to another standard. We're all capable of doing this if we just think about bettering ourselves."

"It's not the notes, it's the rests. The rests are the most important part of music. Without the rests, the notes don't mean anything."

warm-ups for melody 5

Melody 5

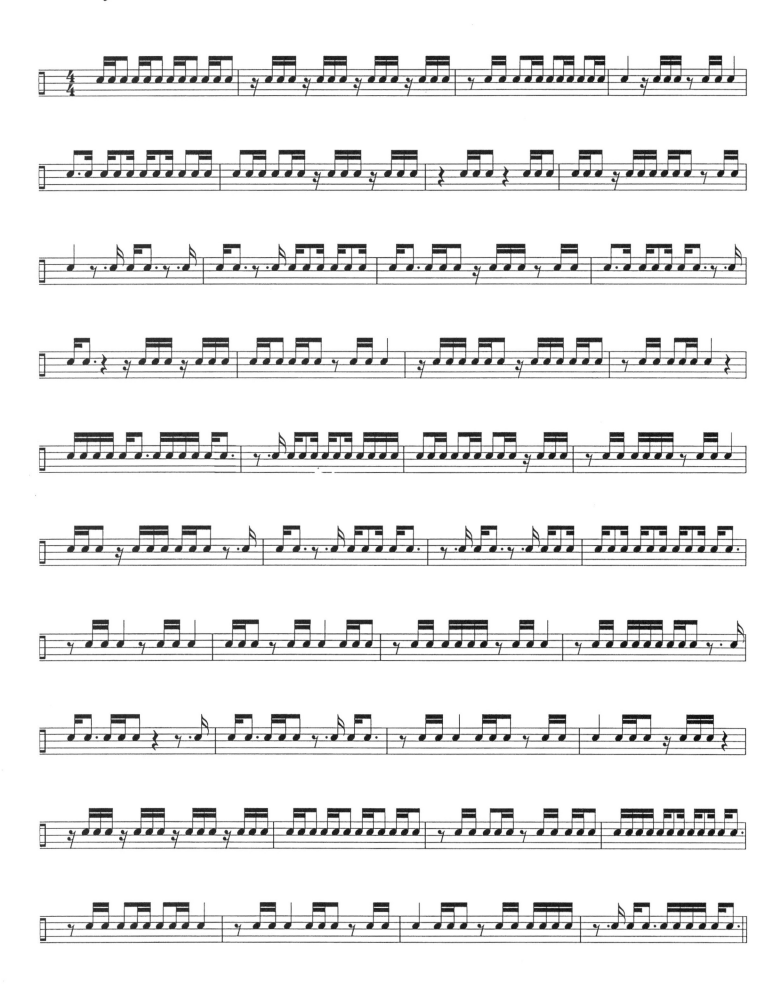

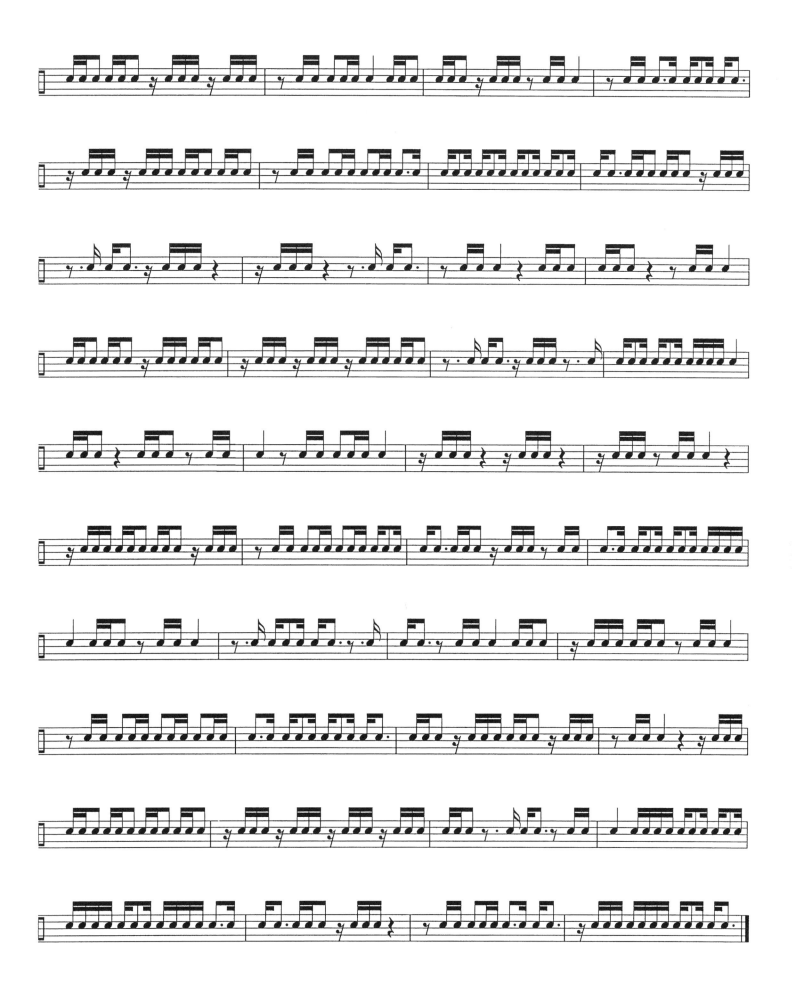

Bonus Melody 1

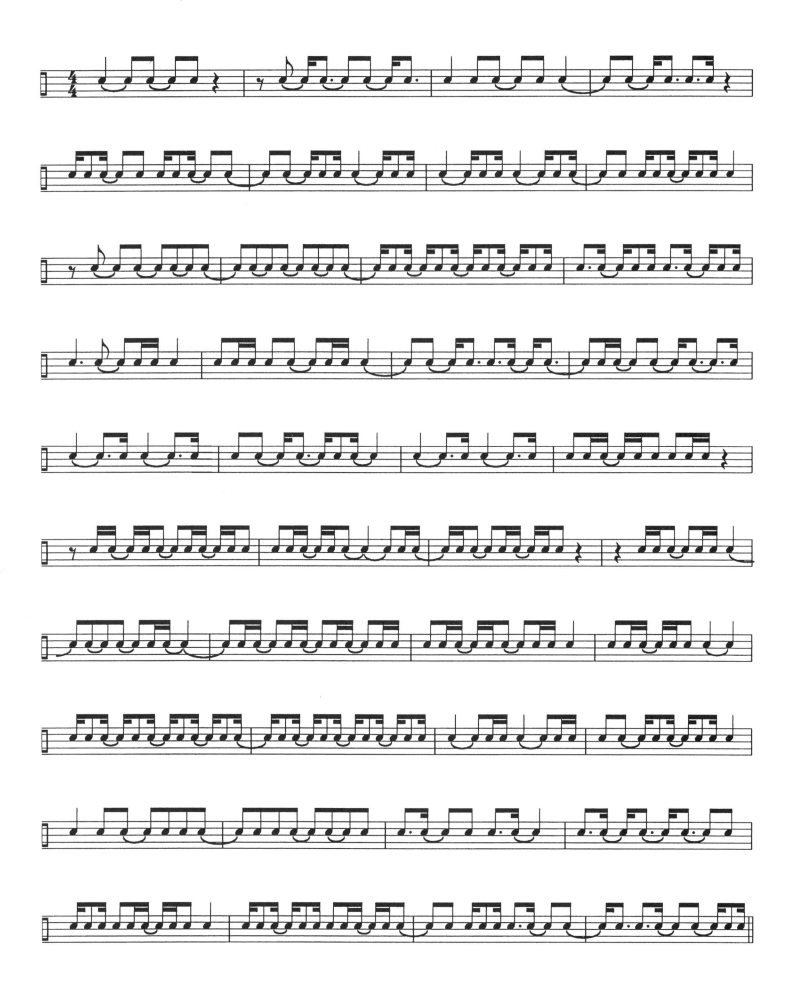

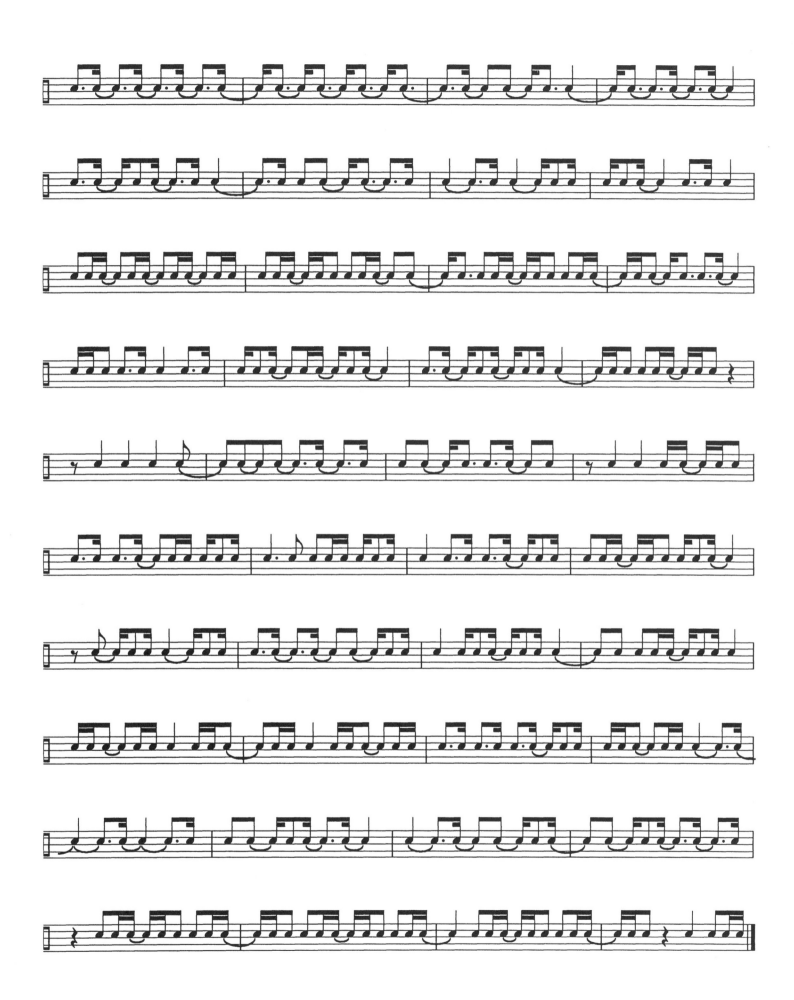

Bonus Melody 2

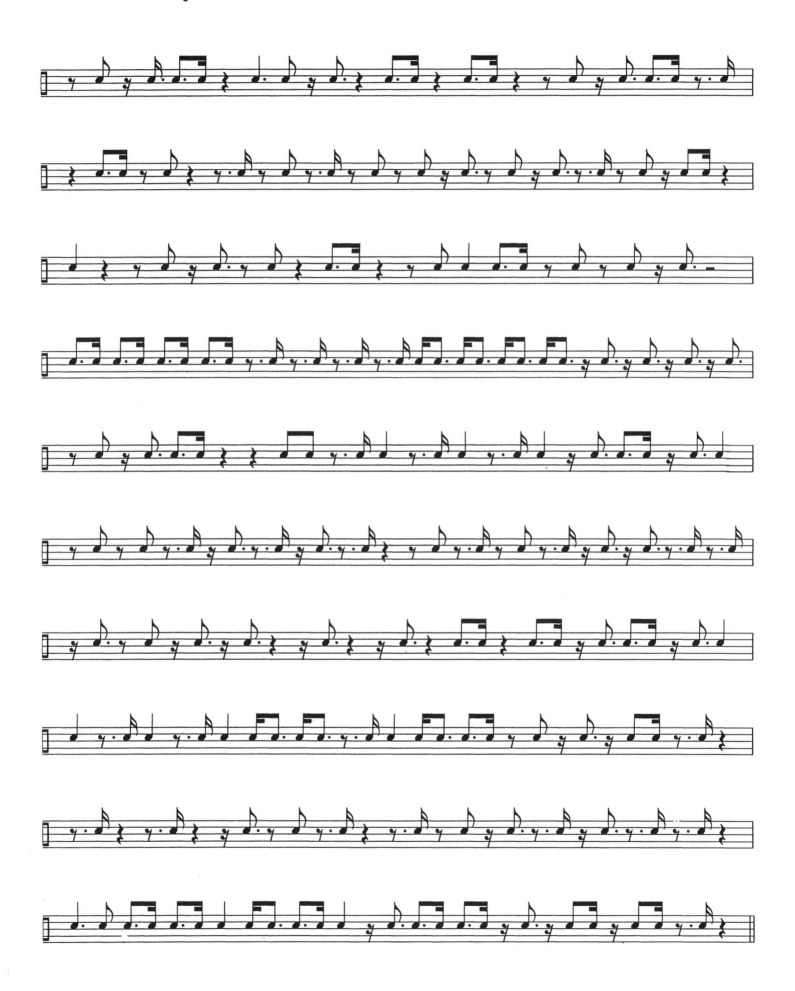

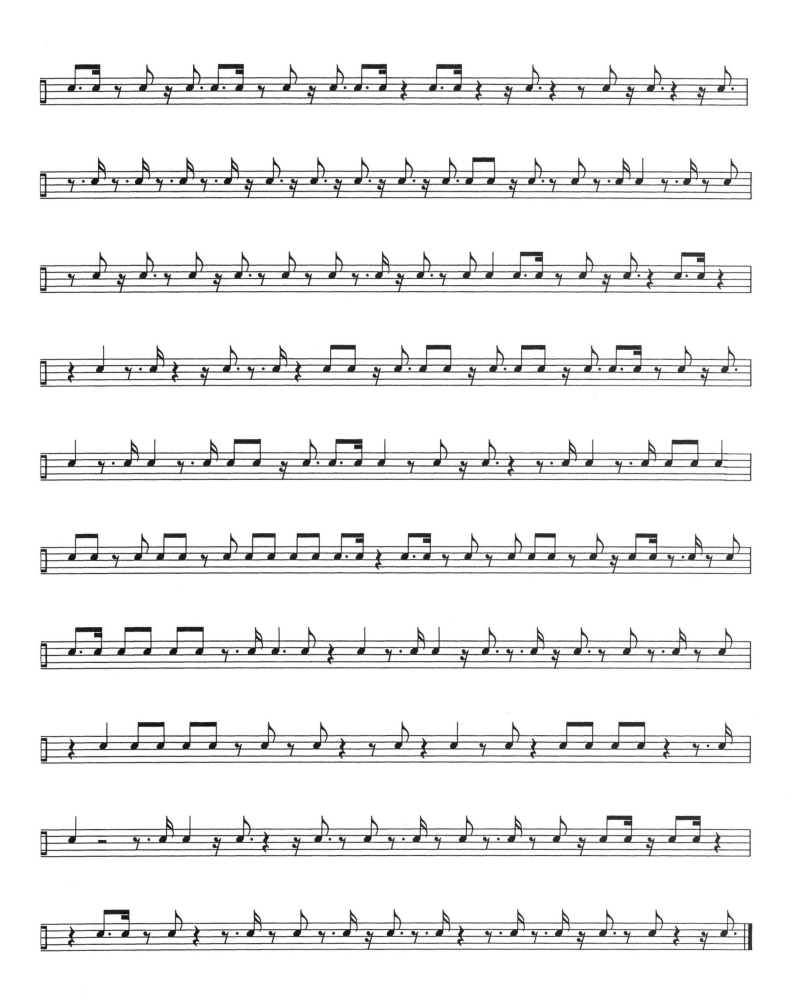

Bonus Melody 3

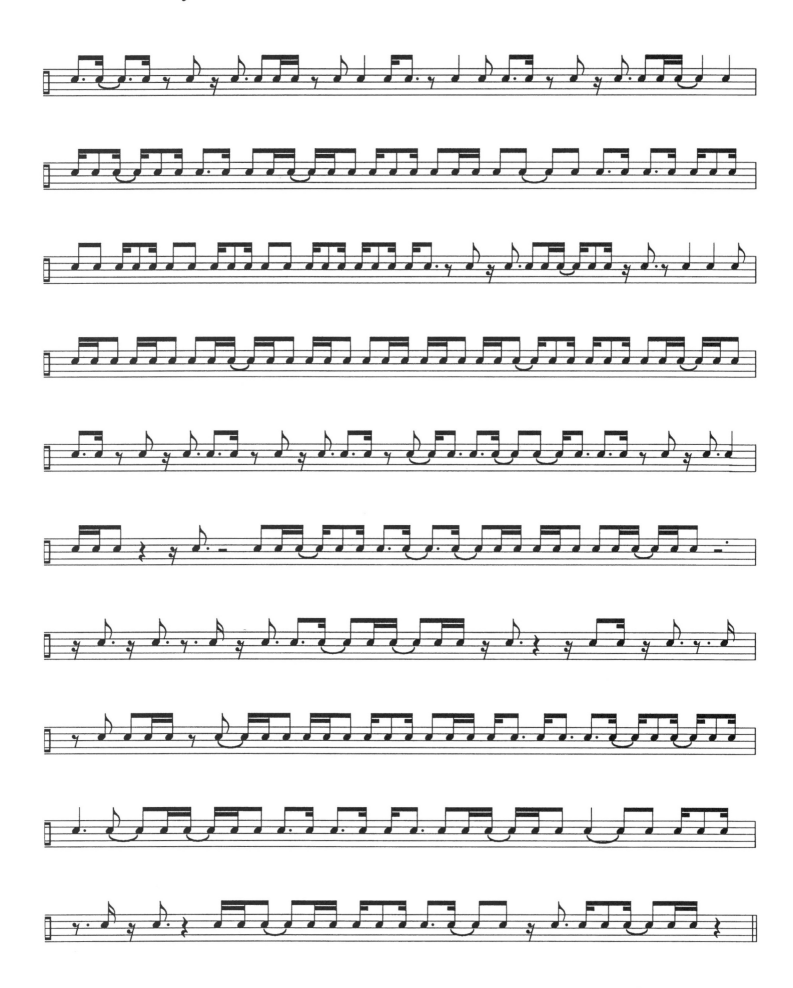

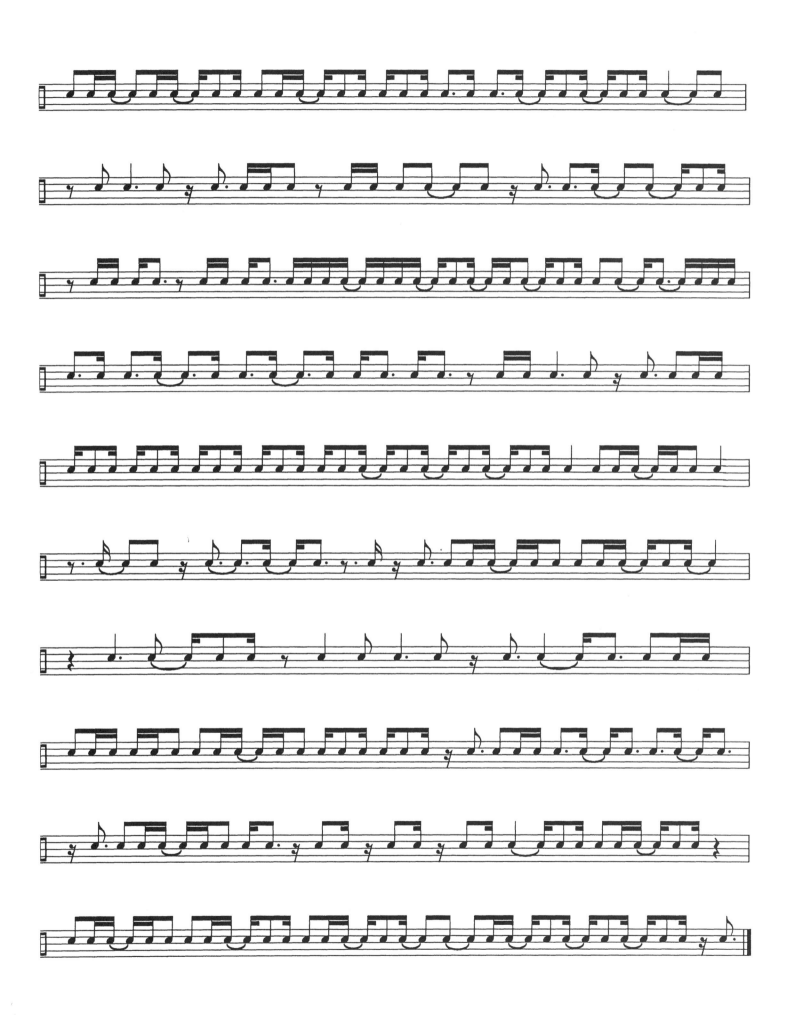

45

PATTERNS

Listed below are some of the rhythmic patterns used throughout the book. These are merely suggestions for one-bar patterns that can be used as one part of a system or bonus. After mastering a bonus with the pattern or patterns shown with that bonus, try substituting one of these patterns or create your own. The possibilities are endless.

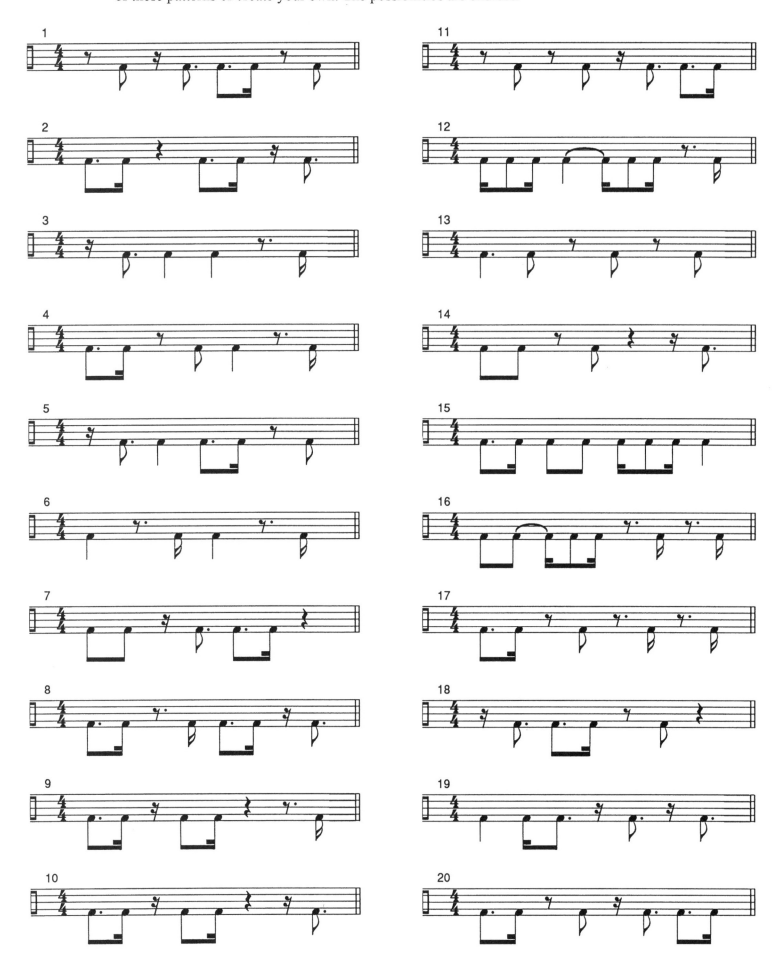

47

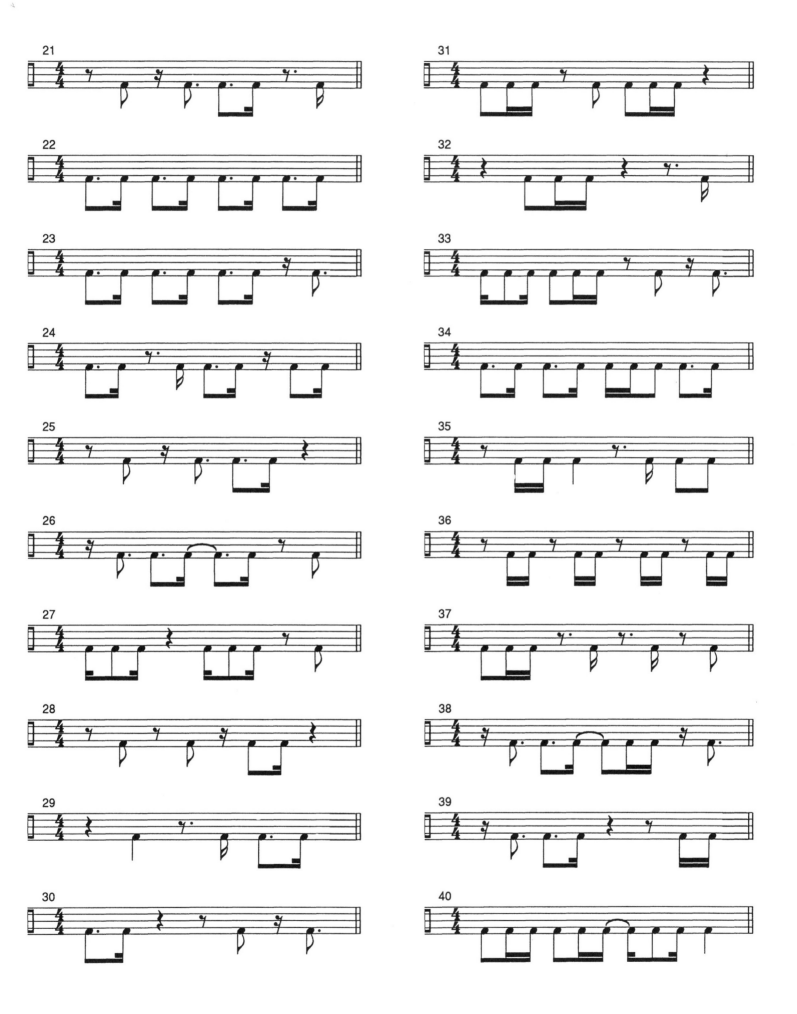

PATTERN EXERCISES

In addition to using the Patterns with systems and bonuses, here are some exercises that you can do using patterns only.

PATTERN EXERCISE #1

INSTRUCTIONS:

<u>Step 1</u>

Turn to Patterns #1 - 10
Play Pattern #1 Broken (play pattern with LH on SN, play rests of pattern with RH on XH)
Example:

Pattern #1

Broken

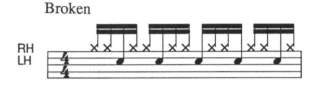

<u>Step 2</u>

Add Upbeats with LF on HH.
Example:

<u>Step 3</u>

While looking at the column of patterns #1 - 10, focus on Pattern #2.
Now, in addition to playing Pattern #1 with hands and upbeats with LF, play Pattern #2 with RF on BD as Melody.
Example:

<u>Step 4</u>

Play this for 4 bars.

Example:

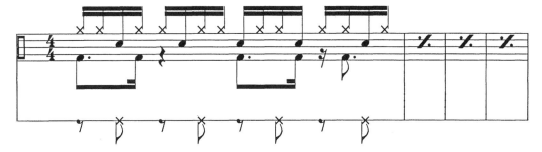

Step 5

Next, proceed down the page (of patterns #1 - 10). Now play Pattern #2 Broken with hands, Pattern #3 with RF on BD, and continue Upbeats with LF.
Example:

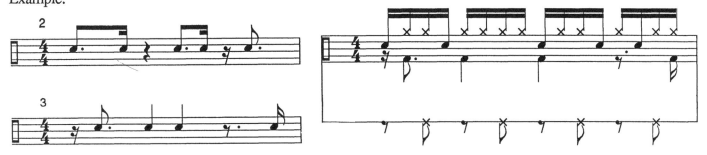

Step 6

Play this for 4 bars.
Example:

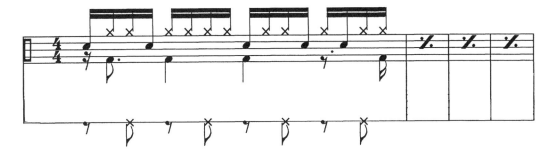

Step 7

Proceed to the next pattern going down the page and continue the same process again and again until you run out of patterns. You can do this with all the columns of patterns.

Step 8

Sing each part you are playing once you have mastered the exercise. Begin first by singing the quarter notes (click).

HINT: Depending on the degree of independence skills you have developed, you may be able to do this Exercise sight-reading down the page, or you may need time to hear each new pattern against each new melody.

Work slowly and patiently, taking one step at a time. Repeat each line as many times as necessary to hear it and play correctly.

Do this exercise first with the right-hand lead (as instructed), and then reverse hands, playing the RH on SN and LH on XH. Also, this exercise can be played with either a straight feel or a swing feel. Try both.

PATTERN EXERCISE #2

Follow all instructions for Exercise #1, but when you get to Step 4, play only 2 bars of pattern and melody before moving on. The same thing applies to Step 6.
Example:

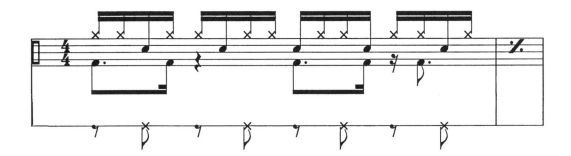

PATTERN EXERCISE #3

Follow all instructions for Exercise #1, but when you get to Step 4, play only 1 bar of pattern and melody before moving on. The same thing applies to Step 6.
Example:

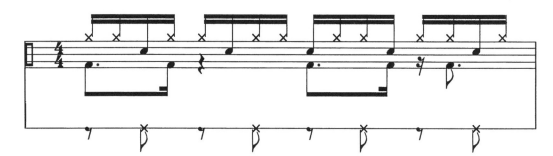

PATTERN EXERCISE #4: THE ULTIMATE CHALLENGE!

Follow all instructions for Exercise #1, but instead of playing Upbeats with the LF as instructed in Step 2, play Pattern #3 with the LF on HH. Now you will be playing three patterns simultaneously. Do this each time you change patterns. As you play down the page, focus on three patterns at once. Patience & Perseverance! Remember to sing all parts once you've mastered the independence.
Example:

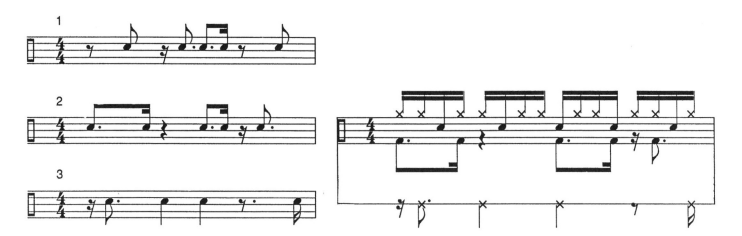

Section II

TRIPLETS AND ODD TIMES

Triplets

In this Section you'll find a variety of Triplet Bonuses followed by Melodies.

The 8th-Note Triplet Bonuses are played as Shuffles, while the 16th-Note Triplet Bonuses are played with a half-time feel. Follow Tempo suggestions.

All of the Triplet Bonuses follow the same basic instructions as those given in Section 1 Bonus Instructions. Any additional instructions are shown prior to specific Bonuses when necessary.

8th-Note Triplet Bonuses

♩ = 70
8th Note triplet melody

MEMORIZE PATTERNS
TURN TO WARM-UPS/MELODY
PLAY PATTERNS WITH MELODY

HINT: All 8th Notes are to be played as *straight 8th notes*. If you aren't used to playing 4 against 3, you should familiarize yourself with that *before* attempting these Bonuses.

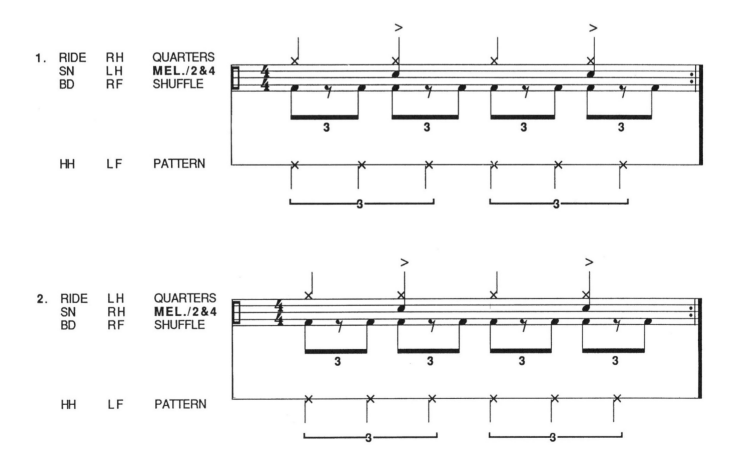

52

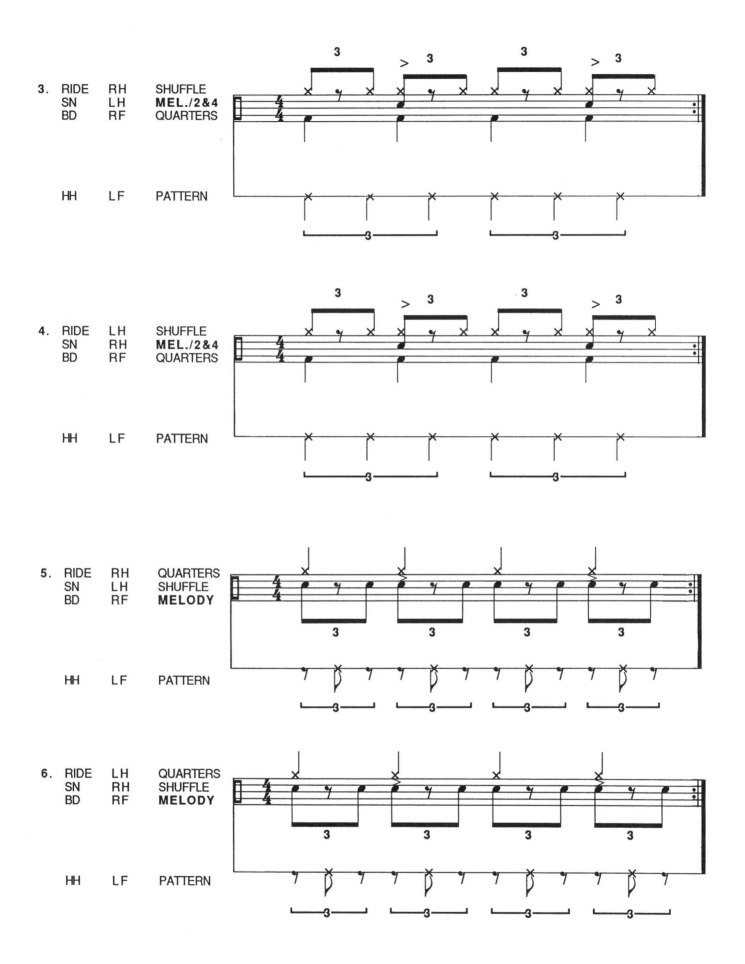

53

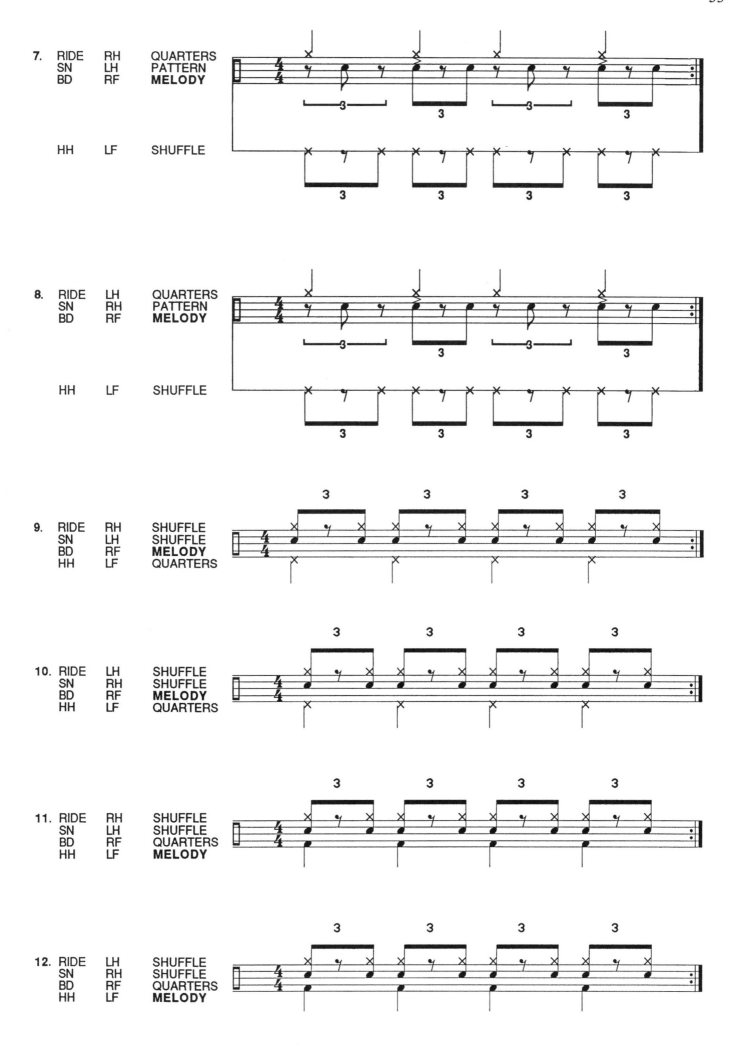

16th-Note Triplet Bonuses

♩ = 60
16th note triplet melody

MEMORIZE PATTERNS
TURN TO WARM-UPS/MELODY
PLAY PATTERNS WITH MELODY

Melody Interpretation: Play Melody with a Swing (Triplet) interpretation. See Example below.

Example:

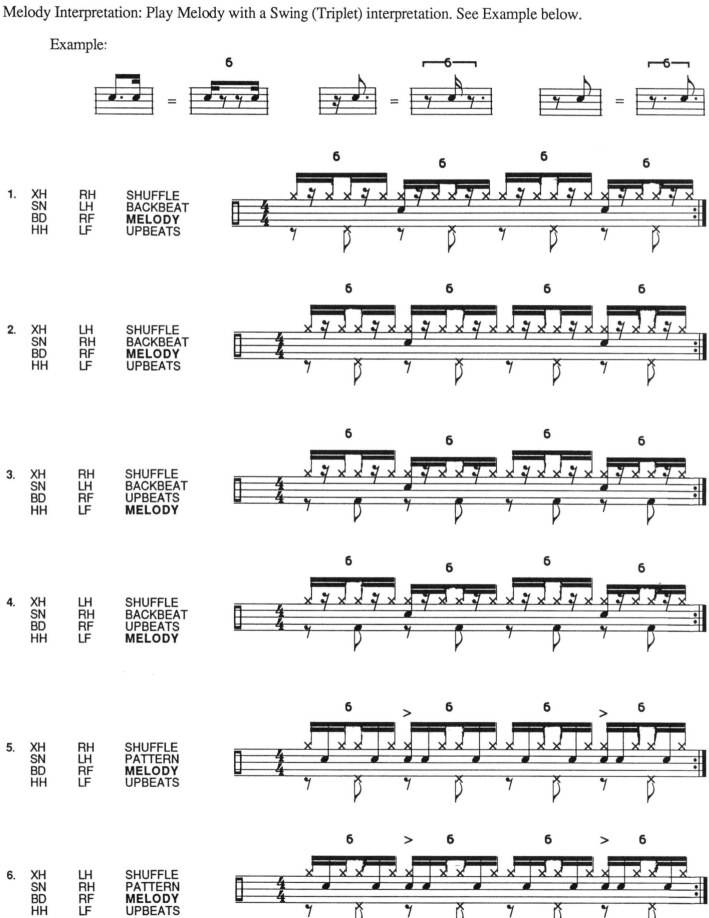

1. XH	RH	SHUFFLE	
SN	LH	BACKBEAT	
BD	RF	**MELODY**	
HH	LF	UPBEATS	

2. XH	LH	SHUFFLE	
SN	RH	BACKBEAT	
BD	RF	**MELODY**	
HH	LF	UPBEATS	

3. XH	RH	SHUFFLE	
SN	LH	BACKBEAT	
BD	RF	UPBEATS	
HH	LF	**MELODY**	

4. XH	LH	SHUFFLE	
SN	RH	BACKBEAT	
BD	RF	UPBEATS	
HH	LF	**MELODY**	

5. XH	RH	SHUFFLE	
SN	LH	PATTERN	
BD	RF	**MELODY**	
HH	LF	UPBEATS	

6. XH	LH	SHUFFLE	
SN	RH	PATTERN	
BD	RF	**MELODY**	
HH	LF	UPBEATS	

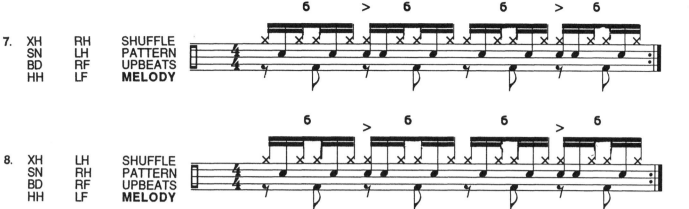

16th-Note Triplet Cross

♩ = 60
16th note triplet melody

ALTERNATE STICKING
MEMORIZE PATTERNS
TURN TO WARM-UPS/MELODY
PLAY PATTERNS WITH MELODY

These Bonuses should be played using what Gary called "Open Arm" approach (RH played on Right XH, LH played on Left XH). This concept is discussed further in Gary's first book, *The New Breed*, on page 4 under "MY APPROACH TO DRUM SETUP: TERRITORIAL RIGHTS."

After mastering all these bonuses using the alternate sticking shown, you can also play them using the *Broken* approach (play melody or pattern with one hand on Snare/Toms, and the rests of the melody or pattern with the other hand on XH or Ride).

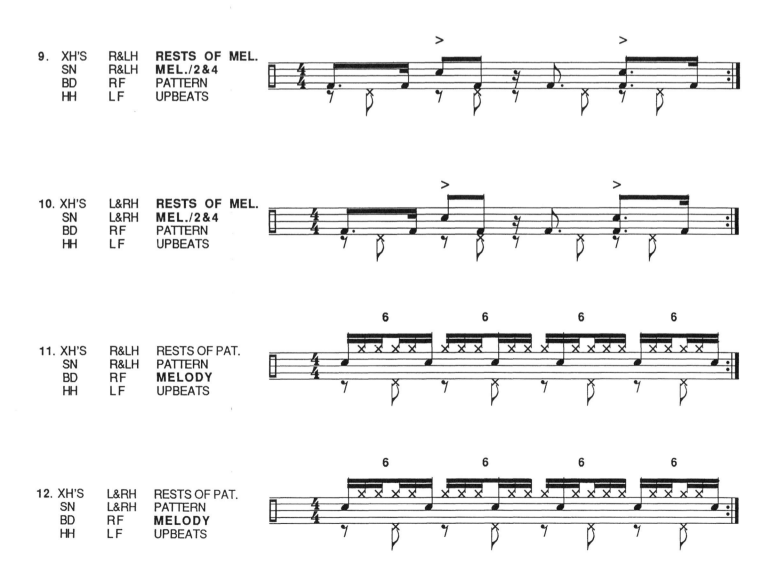

warm-ups for 8th-note triplet melody

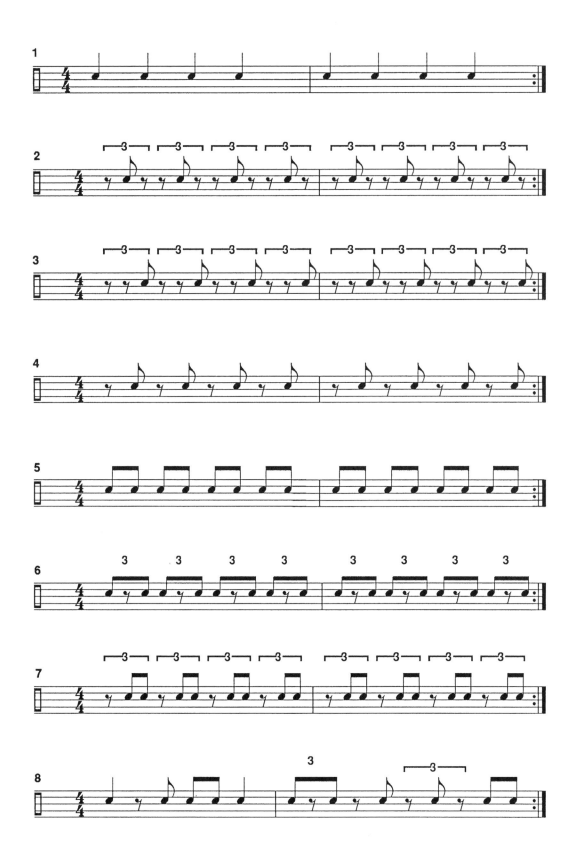

warm-ups for 16th-note triplet melody

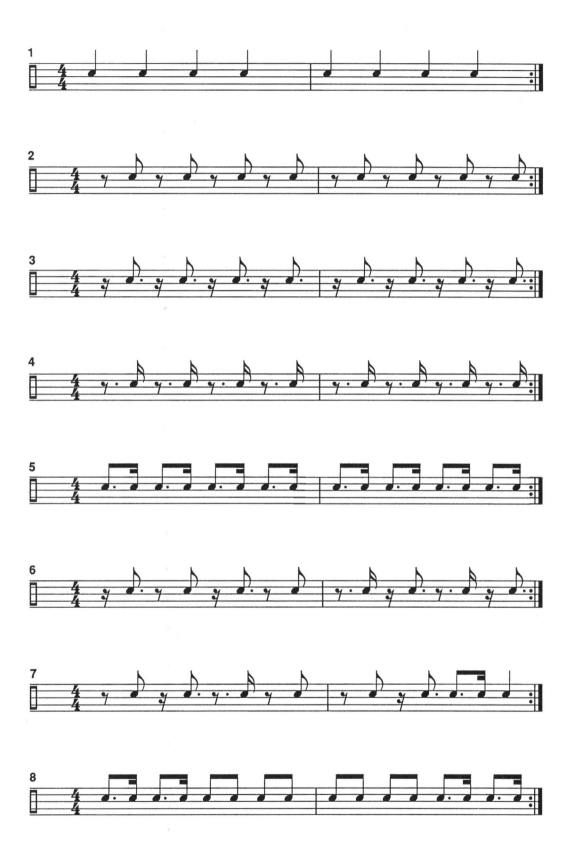

8th-note Triplet Melody

16th-note Triplet Melody

61

Odd Times

Here you'll find groups of odd-time Bonuses followed by Warm-up and Melody for each group. Apply same instructions as those given in Section I Bonus Instructions.

5/8 Bonuses

♩ = 60
5/8 melody

MEMORIZE PATTERNS
PLAY THEM WITH WARM-UPS
PLAY THEM WITH MELODY

1. XH   RH   RIDE PATTERN
   SN   LH   PATTERN
   BD   RF   **MELODY**
   HH   LF   PATTERN

2. XH   LH   RIDE PATTERN
   SN   RH   PATTERN
   BD   RF   **MELODY**
   HH   LF   PATTERN

3. XH   RH   RIDE PATTERN
   SN   LH   **MELODY**
   BD   RF   PATTERN
   HH   LF   PATTERN

4. XH   LH   RIDE PATTERN
   SN   RH   **MELODY**
   BD   RF   PATTERN
   HH   LF   PATTERN

5. XH   RH   RIDE PATTERN
   SN   LH   PATTERN
   BD   RF   PATTERN
   HH   LF   **MELODY**

6. XH   LH   RIDE PATTERN
   SN   RH   PATTERN
   BD   RF   PATTERN
   HH   LF   **MELODY**

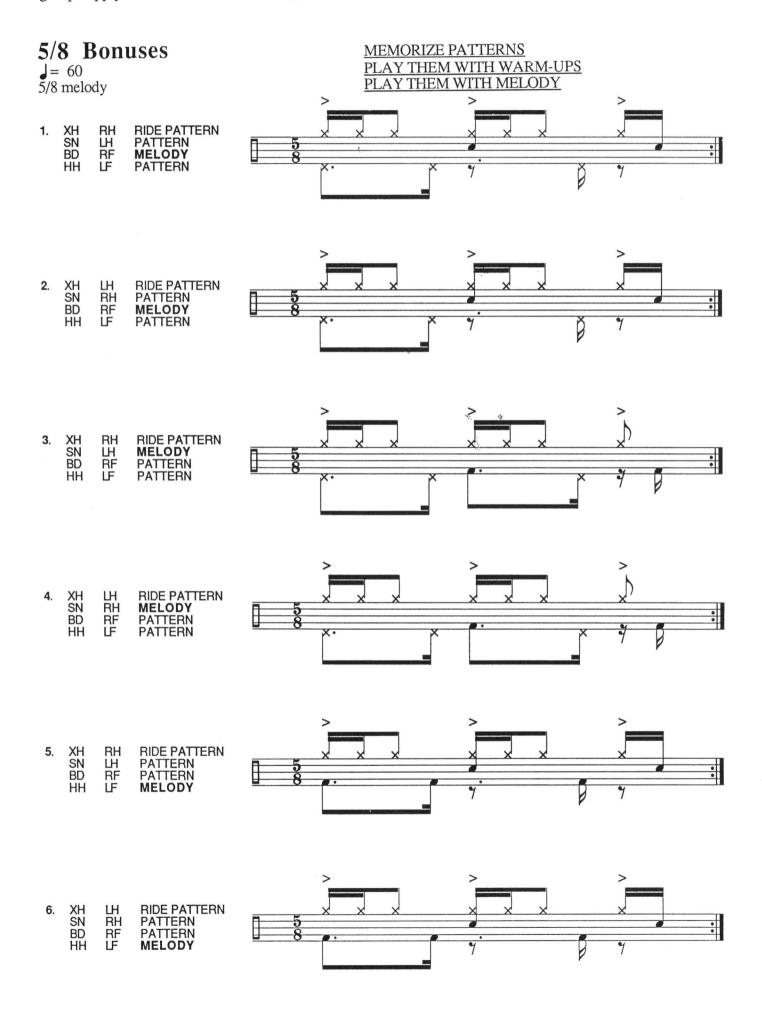

warm-ups for 5/8 melody

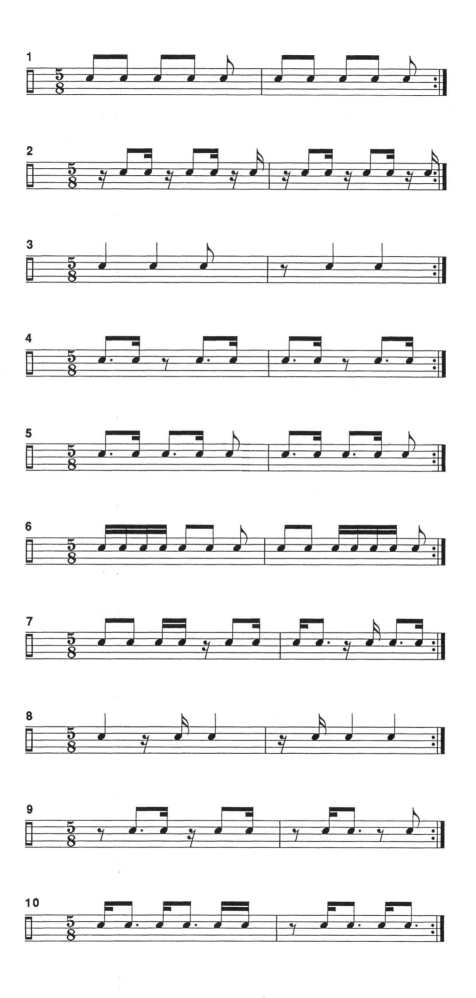

64

5/8 Melody

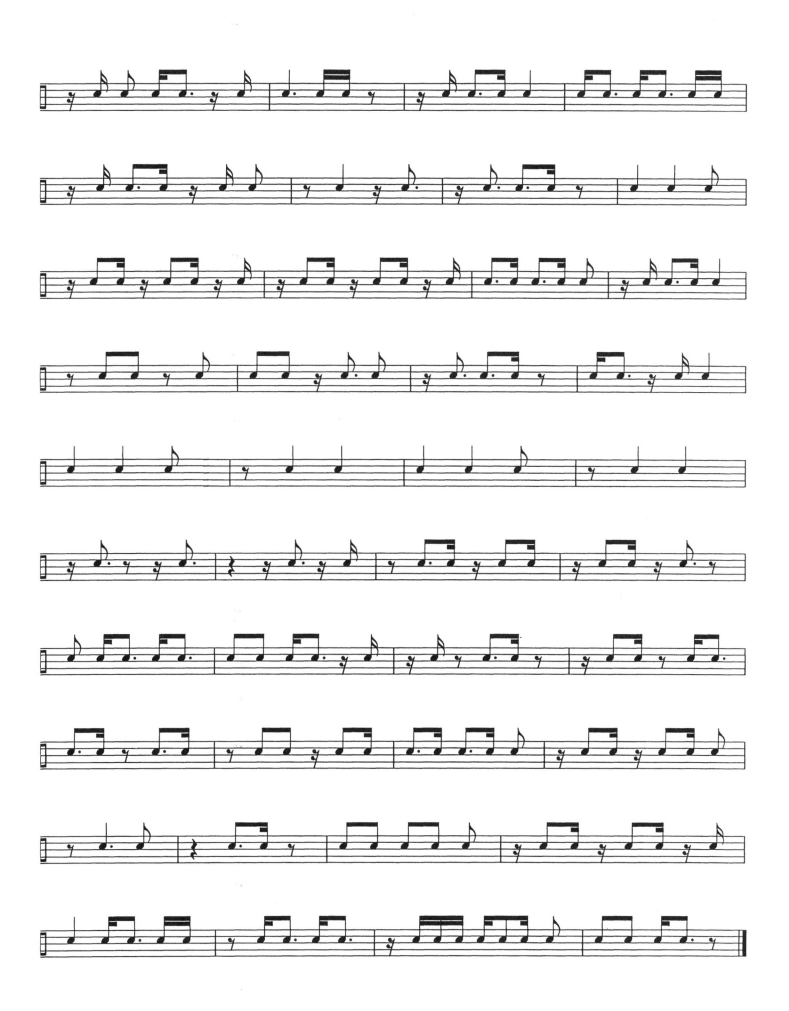

66

7/8 Bonuses

♩ = 60
7/8 melody

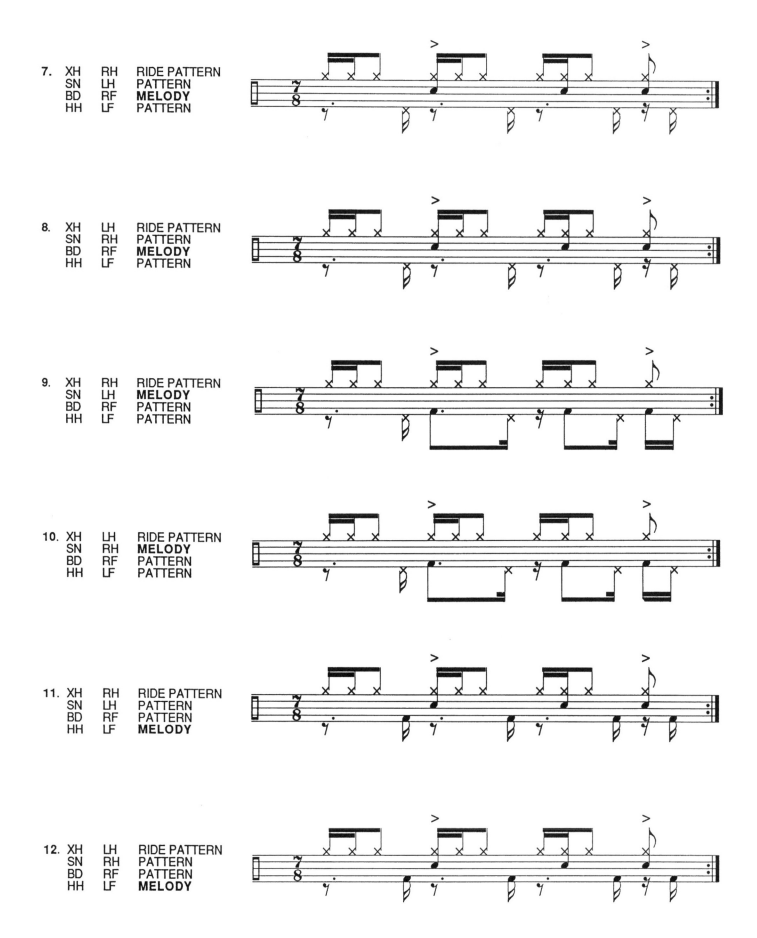

7. XH   RH   RIDE PATTERN
    SN   LH   PATTERN
    BD   RF   **MELODY**
    HH   LF   PATTERN

8. XH   LH   RIDE PATTERN
    SN   RH   PATTERN
    BD   RF   **MELODY**
    HH   LF   PATTERN

9. XH   RH   RIDE PATTERN
    SN   LH   **MELODY**
    BD   RF   PATTERN
    HH   LF   PATTERN

10. XH   LH   RIDE PATTERN
    SN   RH   **MELODY**
    BD   RF   PATTERN
    HH   LF   PATTERN

11. XH   RH   RIDE PATTERN
    SN   LH   PATTERN
    BD   RF   PATTERN
    HH   LF   **MELODY**

12. XH   LH   RIDE PATTERN
    SN   RH   PATTERN
    BD   RF   PATTERN
    HH   LF   **MELODY**

warm-ups for 7/8 melody

68

7/8 Melody

70

6/8 Bonuses
♩. = 60
6/8 melody

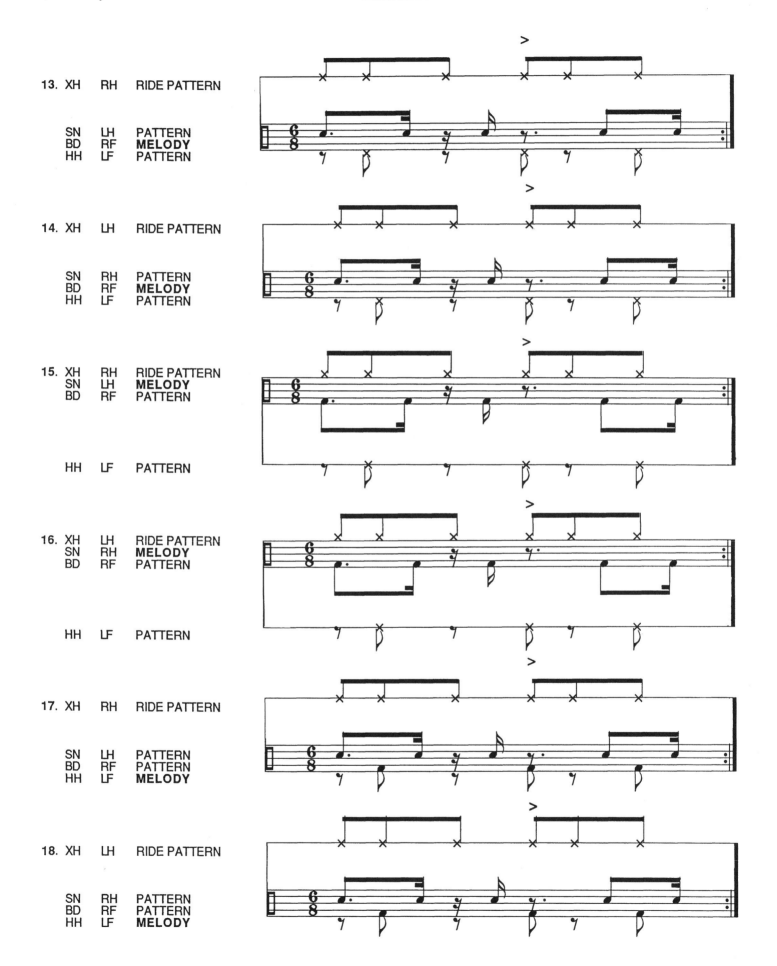

warm-ups for 6/8 melody

72

6/8 Melody

73

12/8 Bonuses

♩. = 60
12/8 melody

MEMORIZE PATTERNS
PLAY THEM WITH WARM-UPS
PLAY THEM WITH MELODY

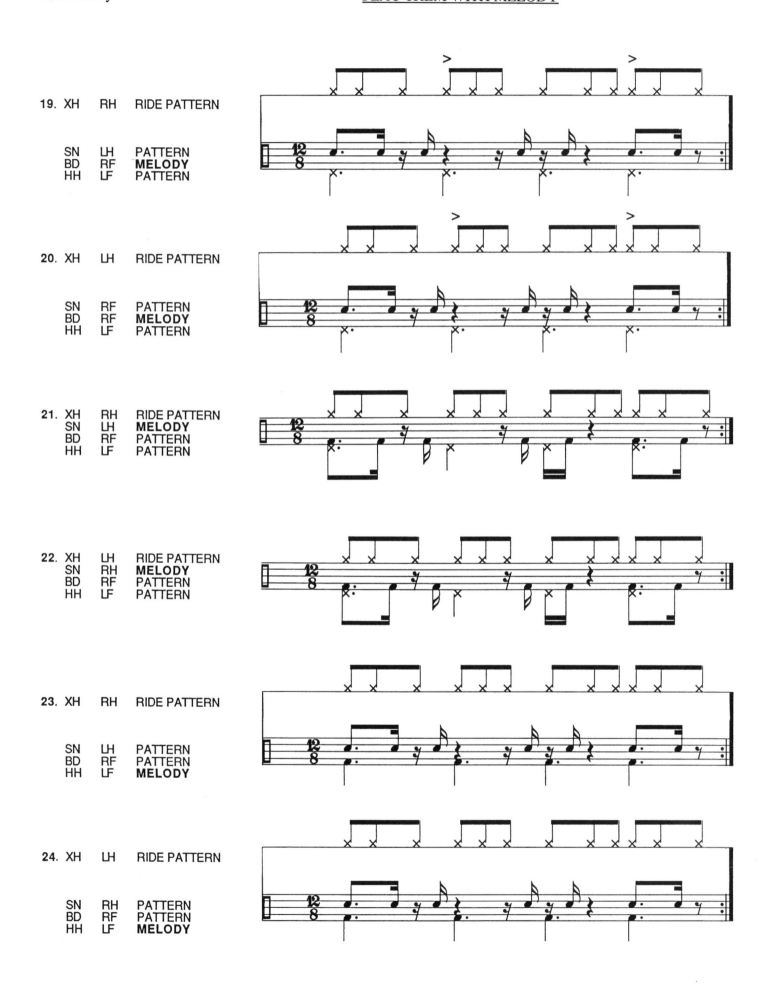

19. XH   RH   RIDE PATTERN

SN   LH   PATTERN
BD   RF   **MELODY**
HH   LF   PATTERN

20. XH   LH   RIDE PATTERN

SN   RF   PATTERN
BD   RF   **MELODY**
HH   LF   PATTERN

21. XH   RH   RIDE PATTERN
SN   LH   **MELODY**
BD   RF   PATTERN
HH   LF   PATTERN

22. XH   LH   RIDE PATTERN
SN   RH   **MELODY**
BD   RF   PATTERN
HH   LF   PATTERN

23. XH   RH   RIDE PATTERN

SN   LH   PATTERN
BD   RF   PATTERN
HH   LF   **MELODY**

24. XH   LH   RIDE PATTERN

SN   RH   PATTERN
BD   RF   PATTERN
HH   LF   **MELODY**

warm-ups for 12/8 melody

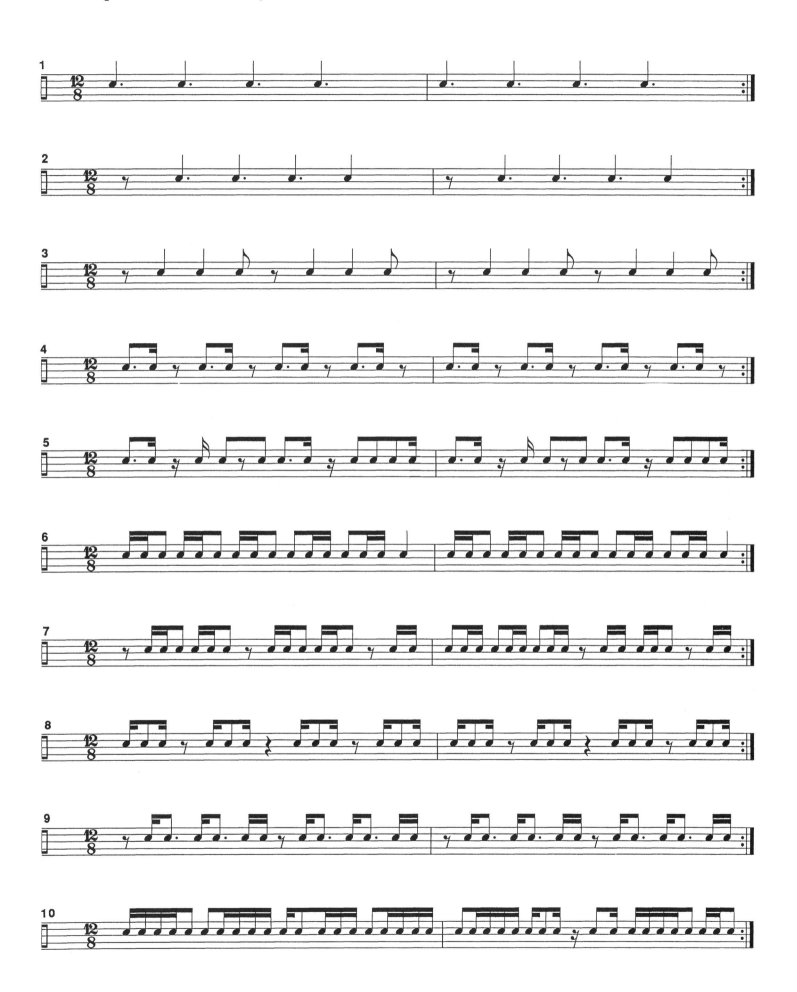

12/8 Melody

Section III

In

Memory and Tribute

to

Gary

Gary meant so very much to so many people. Words can barely express the impact he had on our lives. I can only say, we were the ones who were blessed. We'd like to share some of those feelings here. For all those who didn't know Gary or have the honor of studying or working with him, I hope this may give you a glimpse of his great spirt and character.

Besides being an innovative teacher, Gary was one of the most influential innovators in the music business for nearly two decades (late 1950s - early '70s). His recording credits alone are overwhelming, especially for us "baby boomers" who grew up listening to his inspiring playing nearly every day of our teen years. A modest list of the hits Gary played on is provided in his first book, *The New Breed*.

A few examples include: "Downtown"—Petula Clark; "He's So Fine"—The Chiffons; "Time In A Bottle," "Leroy Brown," "I Love You With A Song"—Jim Croce; "Up On The Roof," "Under The Boardwalk," "Save The Last Dance For Me"—The Drifters; "My Broken Heart," "All Of Me," "Esso Besso,"—Paul Anka; "My Boyfriend's Back"—The Angles; "Lover Come Back," "God Bless The Child"—Aretha Franklin; "It's My Party"—Leslie Gore; "Spanish Harlem," "Stand By Me"—Ben E. King; "Twist and Shout"—The Isley Brothers; "I'm A Believer"—The Monkeys; "Brown Eyed Girl"—Van Morrison; "New York Tendaberry"—Laura Nyro; "Breaking Up Is Hard To Do," "Happy Birthday Sweet Sixteen"—Neil Sedaka; "Remember Walking In The Sand"—Shangri-las; "Walk On By," "I'll Never Fall In Love Again," "Do You Know The Way To San Jose," "Say A Little Prayer," "Make It Easy On Yourself"—Dionne Warwick; "The Boxer"—Simon & Garfunkel; "Promises, Promises," "Alfie,"—Burt Bacharach; "Locomotion"—Little Eva; "Going Out Of My Head"—Little Anthony & The Imperials; "It Hurts To Be In Love"—Gene Pitney; "My Foolish Heart"—Bobby Darin; "Sugar, Sugar"—The Archies; "Blue Velvet," "Please Help Me I'm Falling," "Blue On Blue," "Mr. Lonely"—Bobby Vinton; "Do You Believe In Magic"—Lovin'Spoonful; and the list goes on and on. In total, Gary played on over 12,000 studio dates throughout his career.

An in-depth interview with Gary appeared in the April 1983 issue of *Modern Drummer*. A photocopy of the article can be obtained by contacting the magazine. It's educational and inspiring to say the least. If you haven't had the pleasure, I highly recommend the experience.

Gary felt life had many stages, and though he didn't think he was in the final stage of life, he felt that teaching was his final active musical step. He wanted to capture the imagination of his pupils, fire them up, give them the benefit of his years in the business, bolster their courage, help with insight into their personal and professional hassles and be a true friend and mentor. He loved his pupils, and I feel it was reciprocated.

On a personal note, my favorite recollection is his explanation of why he was so content to work from his home studio: "I spent years on the road, driving through towns at night, seeing a cozy house and through the lighted windows, a family enjoying being together. Now that I've paid my dues, that's what makes me happy—family and home."

Gary really paid his dues—50 years as a working musician. He defined success as "making a living at what you love to do." He was *very successful!*

Janice Chester

Galye's memory of Gary's #1 Philosophy

Pinpoint your goal and dedicate yourself to that goal, leaving behind your superficial desires. Your life must become your goal in order for you to become a success.

Gayle Chester

I'm sitting here crying, reading everything "his children" wrote about him. Every word is true. My father was one of a kind, and I'm grateful to the students for keeping his name more than just a memory.

He was a way of life, and I was brought up by it. He had an uncanny way of knowing what you were feeling and thinking with just one glance. He used to say it was from many years on the road: "You get to know people."

When I think of my Dad, I think of his love, his talent, his dominance, persistence, honesty, understanding compassion and his funny nature. He used to tell me, "When you want something, go for it. You are the only one who's going to get it. It won't come walking up to you."

Music was his life. I remember coming home late at night, and he'd be sitting in the studio, reading or listening to music, drinking coffee and smoking cigarettes. His whole life was rhythm. He walked in rhythm, even coughed in Time. Everything he did was in Time.

He believed that if you worked hard enough for something it would come your way. He used to say, "If you want it bad enough, you can taste it." Success to him was being happy with your life—that's it. You don't have to let everyone know. It just mattered within yourself.

I love you Dad, and your strength will live inside me forever.

Mandy Chester

One of the greatest loves my father and I shared was our love of music. Having shared this while growing up inspired me to do what I do today. It still makes me feel really warm to hear his name mentioned in the studio. He always played a nice bass drum and even today, my favorite recording snare drum is his old wood snare. His contributions will live a lot longer than we will.

Gary Chester, Jr.

Daddy, Oh Daddy

Daddy, oh Daddy I miss you so. You taught me so much, you'll never know.
I kicked and I screamed when things weren't my way, always managing to ruin your hard working day.
I'm sorry for being such a difficult child, but your rules and discipline finally calmed my wild.

As I grew older and moved out on my own, I was all by myself, but never alone.
I heard your words echo loud and clear in my mind, I fought, I rebelled, but I learned in time.
Everyone tries to tell me what's right and what's wrong, but now thanks to you Dad, I've learned to be strong.

Daddy, oh Daddy, you left us behind, without any warning, yet I feel peace of mind.
You were blessed with a talent that so few possess, sharing with those who'd not settle for less.
I'm so proud of you Daddy, you'll never leave, so I'll be happy and try not to grieve.

Daddy, oh Daddy, you'll always be near. I want you to know that my love is sincere.

"Ya' dig?"

I love you.
Jena-mia ("the lump")

Message to daughters

Gary always told them to zero in on one thing, concentrate totally on that. While there are exceptional people who are diverse and excel in many things, it's best to totally immerse yourself in one instrument or one goal. Only by giving it everything you've got can you develop to your *full potential.*

Janice Chester

The degree of my father's strength was based on a foundation of respect through discipline. The attitude that he instilled in regard to one's personal being was given freely to anyone who asked for it. His general philosophy, as a father and a teacher, created a full spectrum of sincerity and application of action.

Music was part of his soul. What he taught in the studio encompassed not only the correct way to play, but the feeling behind it. The teaching of his art was based on his life experience, along with his musical experience. My Dad strongly believed that a marriage must exist between emotional sensitivity and ability, whether applied to music or personal life.

His abstract depth was rarely understood or appreciated by anyone, unfortunately, including himself. What hurts me the most, is that "the son of a bitch" left too soon; we were getting closer, and he was beginning to truly understand himself.

I never loved anybody more.

    . . . until we meet again.

Timmy Gurciullo

To Heaven from Katrina

Dear Daddy,

You're so far away. I just want to touch you again. My memories of you and I are so incomplete. I never showed you all I can be for you. It's so hard for me to go on without you by my side to tell me you love me, to laugh with me as well as at me. To me, Daddy, you are my world. I try so hard to think of what you would say to me at times, good or bad, but I just can't.

I think about the time when I was little and you used to throw pennies on dirt roads and I used to pick them up. You used to tell me they were old Indian pennies. Dad, I always knew they were coming from your pocket, but I just loved the walk and the attention I got from you those special times.

You've inspired me to sing from my heart and soul, to *live* from my heart and soul. I listen to all the same music you do. I listen to all the same inspirations. My room is covered with my Daddy. I don't ever want to lose you.

My singing is going really good but I don't feel it's enough for you to be proud of me like you are of your students. I just want you to love me like you do them. I want you to smile at me and tell me what to do.

I'll never forget the look in your eyes when you talked to me about my music, or when I sang for you and a tear fell from your eye. I did that to you—no one else. I want you to be with me, just so I know you're there.

There are so many mixed up feelings inside. Everyone misses you so much. There will never be another you in my life, only what's left in my heart of our special times.

I promise you one thing: your name will live on forever. I'm gonna find my road to follow and I know deep in my heart that you'll be holding my hand.

I'll always love you Daddy. Please don't stop loving me or ever forget me.

You are my total inspiration.

Your daughter,
Katrina Janell Chester

Part of the wonder of knowing Gary included experiencing the most comfortable feeling of being myself, completely, with no restrictions or limitations. I think the longer you live, the more you begin to realize that that experience alone is rare. I miss him terribly, but I have so many great memories and they're as fresh as ever. I feel so grateful to have all that.

I miss his honesty, his directness, and his willingness to listen. He had the patience and concern of a loving parent and an open, child-like spirit that allowed him to be your closest friend. I miss his voice, his sense of humor, his stories, his jokes, his laugh...and his walk.

I miss his confidence, his strength—and his Time. It makes me smile to remember him sitting behind his desk slammin' those quarter notes with his stick on that big old black ashtray. His Time was so beautiful.

I miss the enthusiasm and excitement his energy created. I miss the comradeship he brought out in his students, but he left us that. He left us each other. I have some life-long friends among them, and that makes me happy.

I miss his guidance, his instincts, and his dedication to his work. I miss his old house, the drive up there, his studio, the great side porch, and especially the talks we had out there.

I miss the discipline that studying with him demanded. I miss the encouragement of a wonderful teacher. I miss the love and trust of a great friend.

I miss Gary.

Chris Adams

On August 17, 1987, an entire family of drummers lost their mentor. Gary Chester was that miraculous individual who, out of love for what he did, gathered such a huge *breed* of people called the Gary Chester Family.

Not many people had the opportunity to really know Gary. Many people heard him play, but few had the chance to talk with him. The fact is that you really didn't need to speak with him to know him. Just listen to any record he ever cut (his favorite was "Mr. Bassman" by Johnny Cymbal) and his personality will appear. In·every groove, you can hear the love and enormous compassion delivered from his soul.

Gary was a natural-born innovator. He was also the most honest person I ever met. He would express his opinion of you to your face, whether you wanted to hear it or not. His inner peace and security gave him the ability to take chances and really create. Gary also had a tremendous sense of humor, and he used this as a tool to make people feel comfortable with him.

Gary Chester was the prime example of a perfect drummer. His enormous love for his instrument combined with his talent allowed him the flexibility to fit into any playing situation. Gary was just as happy recording a soft maraca part with a sand-filled ashtray as he was playing a complex drumset part. He could do anything, and there was no ego involved.

His time was remarkable. He used to say that he had a built-in quarter note. One time we were sitting outside, and he showed me how to keep time to the chirping of birds.

On top of this was his incredible love for mankind He took pride in figuring out why people felt the way they did. He understood the way people reacted to situations, and he used that knowledge to get the most from them— or sometimes just to have a good laugh.

All of this is what made Gary such a fantastic teacher. He made it his business to get inside of every student's head. He got involved with everything: their families, religious beliefs, hobbies, girlfriends and boyfriends, investments, money management, and even their sexuality—the things that were most important to them. He believed that these ingredients within people's lives *directly* influenced the way they sounded on their instrument. Gary believed that your instrument was an extension of yourself. If any part of your life was screwed up, you wouldn't sound good on the drums, no matter how good your chops were. Feel, to him, was everything to a drummer. If you didn't feel right—if you were mad, jealous, upset, afraid—it would show in your playing.

I once went into a lesson smiling and grinning, and really anxious to play. I had only played about two bars when Gary stopped me and said, "What the f*** is bothering you?" He was so tuned in to me that he guessed that I'd had a fight with my girlfriend before the lesson. Gary got very involved with everyone's personal life and was always there to talk to when you needed him.

Gary also demanded respect from every player. There was no jealousy or envy allowed among his students. The 15-year-old high school students were just as important to him as the heavy studio cats he taught. Because of this, the students constantly socialized, shared gigs, and exchanged information about the business with each other. Every year, Gary threw a party with all of his students and friends. He'd buy the beer and food, and help set up the drums. His "children," as he called us, would play his systems, trade solos, tell jokes, and have a great time together. We would all sit around him, and he would talk to us about the true meaning of success. Gary would explain that success was simply the product of working hard, loving what you do, and being the best that you possibly can be.

There was not one student who did not feel a terrible loss when Gary died. We all refuse to accept the fact that Gary is gone, and we have vowed to immortalize his teaching by continuing to learn from his systems and share this knowledge with others.

Corey Christopher Roberts

Reprinted from *Modern Drummer* magazine with permission.

from students...

For me, it's about control. From the control over what you think you're playing (the mental process), to the control over what you're actually playing (the physical process). The idea is to connect the two. Once you begin to develop this control of mind and body, you begin to realize how limitless the possibilities are musically. This is only the beginning!

Jess Wheeler

Gary's Systems can aid improvement in areas that reach far beyond drumming. As much as these exercises can aid one's drumming technically, they are unparalleled in improving one's concentration, the key to most everything we do.

Peter Wilson

Gary's Method is the most sophisticated way to learn to play the drums. It helps you develop your own personality and creativity. But more than that, it's a whole philosophy that becomes part of your life.

To get the possibility to study with a genius like Gary was one of my greatest experiences in life. It changed not only my playing, but also my way of thinking and my attitude in terms of life, business, and relations to people.

You should study this Method with a teacher, because most of the time the exercises are so difficult that only the faith in your teacher gives you the patience and perseverance that you need to reach your goal.

To study with Chris Adams through cassette correspondence is a wonderful way to learn this Method. It's much more than sending a check and getting some independence exercises; it's like having a drumming love affair.

Robert Strobel
Germany

Studying Gary's Systems taught me not only the coordination independence I was looking for, but my Time, reading, and awareness improved dramatically, while showing me a method of learning that has positively affected all aspects of my life.

Mike Ricciardi

The advanced coordination that I developed through studying Gary's Systems is second only to the balance that I obtained between my heart and soul. It was a very spiritual journey that I took with Gary, and I miss him a lot.

Bobby Kent

The secret to mastering these systems is in your lifestyle. The same amount of desire, concentration, relaxation, and confidence needed to play them must be applied to everything in your life. Gary always said, "You can play absolutely anything you want to." By leading me through his lessons, he showed me he was right.

Robert Bond

Gary's Method is the most important thing I've learned since I started playing drums. It opened up my ears so I could hear the whole band at once. It has helped my Time immensely and forced me to really practice and discipline myself. I am thrilled that Chris Adams has continued teaching what my best friend and teacher has given me.

Jonathan Lichtig

Gary's lessons included guidance in handling yourself as a musician and help in directing you towards your future. Here are some of his suggestions that I recall:

"Go out and listen to music, see what's happening out there and how you fit in. Introduce yourself to other musicians; they can be helpful to you. At a club, ask if you can sit in. Find out where jam sessions are and go to them; let people hear you, and listen to others, learn from them.

"Hang out with other drummers; you can be an inspiration to one another. Get into a situation where you're with good players, preferably musicians better than yourself; that'll make you work harder. If you're too good for a band, get into a better one. Be professional: when you're ready to leave a group, try to find a replacement.

"Learn something from every good or bad situation you're in; use it to your advantage. Get paid for what you do. Don't allow anyone who's coming from their own insecurities to put you down."

Gary never dwelled on the negative—"You want that gig? Well, go get it! Can't play that? You got two arms, two legs, and a brain, so what's the problem!"

He was the best audience to play for. He never lied to you about whether you sounded good or bad. That honest reaction is what taught me to trust myself and enabled ideas to flow.

The last thing I learned from Gary was that you can't wait in life; there were so many things I wanted to ask him, but I put them off.

That's just a little bit about Gary and what I learned from him. Boy was I lucky!

Doreen Holmes

Through my years of study with Gary, I learned the importance of Time. The first step to playing good Time is understanding it. Practicing with a click track while studying with Gary gave me a greater awareness of Time. I learned to respect it. I knew exactly where the quarter note was and how all the other notes related to it. By singing the quarter notes, I developed a strong internal pulse.

Gary's Method is the ultimate in coordination, control, focus, awareness, and sensitivity. Singing the various parts of each System made me aware of every note I played. My dynamics improved tremendously. Gary also taught me how to express myself on my instrument. He believed that the instrument was merely an extension of yourself.

I'll always be grateful for the years I spent with that unique individual known as Gary Chester.

Paul Paitchell

Gary would always say that he wasn't teaching how to play drums. He was teaching exercises that would enable drummers to maximize their abilities and creativity. The Systems that Gary developed offer endless possibilities to do both, and are much more than a series of difficult coordination exercises. They require an open mind, the ability to listen, patience, determination, and sensitivity.

Through Gary I learned that to grow as a drummer, you had to grow as a person. They are a reflection of one another. I learned that success isn't necessarily fame, it's developing the attributes mentioned above, having faith in yourself, and trusting your ability.

David Bell

closing notes...

As I complete this book I find myself feeling as though an extremely powerful, innovative, ahead-of-its-time method has finally been completely documented—left for all those who follow, and who will take it from here and go on and on. That was a wish of Gary's, which I assured him I understood, and would do my best to help see that it continued.

I'm proud to have been a part of this. I'm honored to have worked with, studied with, and enjoyed the loving friendship of such a truly great human being as Gary Chester. I laughed with him, cried with him, and learned from him, as I still do.

Shortly after he died and I had just begun writing this book, I remember wondering if he would be near to help me. There were times I was on my own, but there were also times that I felt him look in on me, and sometimes even share a moment.

He left plenty, as if he either planned well in advance or somehow has been able to give a sign when he's most needed. I can honestly say that there were many signposts for me to follow. He's given me so much, as he has to so many others.

I can't help but think that the most rewarding thing for Gary would be for each of us, in our own way, to take it one step further—to make it a part of us.

Chris Adams

"There are a lot of great drummers, but stopping there is not where it's at. You can all go further. If you stop learning and progressing, you'll end up playing weddings and bar mitzvahs. If that's what you want, great, and that's what usually happens. You can make pretty good money, but if you lean on that, and let your learning process diminish, you pay a high price.

"That's what's bad about this business. You don't realize what potentials you have, and you're not tapping those potentials. In order to be successful in this business, you have to be innovative. You've got to give me something that this guy can't give me or that guy can't give me. Otherwise, who the hell needs you? If you're good, you don't know how good you are. There's so much to learn—so much to learn it's not even funny, and wasting time is not going to do it.

"Playing good is not good enough. You've got to be **innovative***."*

Gary Chester

Glossary

Attitude: As defined in the Funk & Wagnall Standard Desk Dictionary: State of mind, behavior or conduct regarding some matter, as indicating opinion or purpose.

Bonus: A term referring to Gary's more advanced exercises.

Broken: A Bonus where one hand (or foot) is playing a Pattern or Melody on one instrument (snare drum in the example below) while the other hand (or foot) is playing the rests of that Pattern or Melody on another instrument (X-hat in the example below).
Example:

Click: The Quarter Note Pulse of a metronome, drum machine, or sequencer used while practicing the Systems or Bonuses.

Cross: A Bonus in which all 16th notes are played alternately between the right and left hands in an open-arm position.

Example:

Disco: Bonuses with a disco feel.

Innovate: As defined by Funk & Wagnall: To introduce or bring in (something new). To bring in new ideas, methods, etc.

Master: As defined by Funk & Wagnall: 1. One exceptionally gifted or skilled in an art, science, etc. 2. To become expert in.
Also: To achieve a level of skill so great as to totally satisfy oneself. Physical, mental, and spiritual contentment.

Melody: The pages of reading material to be played with each System or Bonus.

Pattern: A specific arrangement of rhythmic notes of one or more bars played repeatedly with a System or Bonus.
Examples:
Bass line pattern

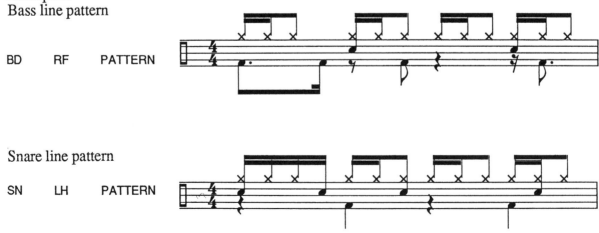

Snare line pattern

Rests: The 16th notes other than those used in a Melody or Pattern.

Example:

```
XH    LH    RESTS of PAT.
SN    RH    PATTERN
```

Singing: To verbally mimic each part that you are playing using a sound that resembles that of each particular instrument. Don't count numbers; just sing syllables. For example, when singing quarter notes you might imitate the sound of the Click, singing "ah, ah, ah, ah...." In singing the hi-hat part, you might use a short sound such as "chick," "chit," or just a short, staccato "ah."

System: One of Gary Chester's basic exercises.

Time: As defined by Funk & Wagnall: The general concept, relation, or fact of continuous or successive existence, capable of division into measurable portions, and comprising the past, present, and future.

> As applied to playing:
> On top of the beat: Ahead of time; early.
> Center of the beat: At the same time; exact.
> Behind the beat: Behind time; late.

Wac-A-Chuck: Gary's term referring to a specific ride pattern.
> Example:

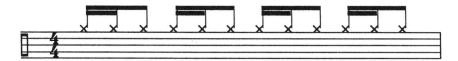

X-hat: Auxiliary closed hi-hat. To use Gary's method most fully, it is recommended that you use two X-hats, one on either side of the kit.

"I know it's hard to stay motivated when you've been in your cellar practicing and practicing, and you go out to a concert and hear a guy who doesn't play half as good as you, and he's making $5,000 a week. So what?! It doesn't make any difference. Your motivation has got to be straight ahead. Your goals have got to stay visible. Nothing must interfere with your practicing or with your love of drumming.

"If you're in this business to be famous, or to pick up chicks, or to get high, or to party—get the f*** out. Because you're not going to get anywhere. It's you. You're doing this for yourself, and if you don't do better for yourself, you're not going to make it."

"You strive to be good. But to be good is not good enough. You've got to be better."